THE TENTH MUSE:

Women Poets Before 1806

Jean Buyze

A Rediscovery of 540 Women Poets
Lost to History

for my best friend Don

Some say there are nine muses; how careless they are!
Behold Sappho of Lesbos is the tenth!

Plato

THE TENTH MUSE: Women Poets Before 1806
Copyright (c) by Jean Buyze, 1980.
All rights reserved.

ISBN: 0-915288-39-7

SHAMELESS HUSSY PRESS
box 3092
berkeley, california 94703

This Index includes women poets from the beginning of literature to the year 1806. Elizabeth Barrett Browning was born in 1806. She seems to be the first major female poet judging by the inclusion of her work in many anthologies. There has been lots of research, publication and literary criticism of poets from the nineteenth and twentieth centuries, but little is known about poets before that time. There are 540 women poets entered in this Index who were born on or before 1806.

This Index is only a beginning. There are more poets out there in the library stacks. Given researchers and time to work, this list could easily be doubled. The information here is often sketchy but that should not imply that that is all there is to know about any particular poet. Much more work needs to be done before we can be reasonably sure we know our literary history and women's history in general. Hopefully, the information here will inspire other women to explore the tomes and tombs for information on early women poets.

Books referred to often in the text will be found in one of the two bibliographies at the end of the Index. One list contains anthologies of women's poetry and the other, biographical dictionaries of women. A book such as Sarah Josepha Hale's *Women's Record* is especially valuable. Not only does it contain biographies of 2,500 women, but also includes poetry and prose of the writers.

Sources for individual poets will be furnished upon receipt of a request and self addressed stamped envelop from the editor, Jean Buyze, 1572 Pearl Street, Benton Harbor, Michigan, 49022.

ACCIAIOLI, MAGDALEN;   died 1610, Florence, Italy.
Work: poems.
She was a favorite of Christina, Duchess of
Tuscany.

ACCOMPLISHED MAID FROM TUSCANY: fl. 13th century,
Florence, Italy. a.k.a. La Compiuta Donzella,
The Divine Sibyl, The Perfect Maid.
Work: three sonnets remain.
She was the first woman poet of talent to
write in a modern European language; accord-
ing to her poetry she did not want to be
forced to marry, or to marry at all.

ACCORAMBONI, VITTORIA: 1557-1585, Gublio and
Padua, Italy.
Work: poems.
She was married at sixteen to Perrétti. Her
lover, Orsini, murdered his wife and had her
husband murdered by Vittoria's brother. A
Medici then murdered Orsini, was brought to
trial and strangled in prison. Her brother
was beheaded for his crimes. She is the sub-
ject of a play, *The White Devil, or Vittoria
Corombona*, 1612.

ACKERE, MARIA VAN (nee DOOLAEGHE): 1803-1884,
Belgium.
Work: *Aan de Belgische Dichters*, 1833; *Made-
lieven*, 1840; *De Avondlamp*, 1850; *Winter-
bloemen*, 1868; *Najaarsvruchten*, 1869; *Vereen-
igde Dichtwerken*, 1876.

ADAMS, JEAN or JANE: 1710-1765, Renfrewshire,
Scotland.
Work: *Miscellany Poems by Mrs. Jane Adams*,
1734, Glasgow.
She educated herself while working as a maid
for a minister; her religious poems were pub-
lished by subscription; she then opened a
school for girls but had money problems; the
unsold copies of her book were shipped to
Boston and never heard about again; she had
to close the school; died in a poor house.

ADAMS, SARAH FULLER (nee FLOWER): 1805-1848,
Essex, England.
Work: *Vivia Perpetua*, 1841, a long dramatic

poem about Christianity. *Hymns*, set to music
by her sister, Eliza Flower. *The Royal Pro-
gress*, 1845; a ballad.
She was a devout Unitarian; her most famous
hymn, *Nearer My God to Thee*, caused a reli-
gious controversy as it contained no direct
reference to Jesus.

ADELWIP: popular name in Germany for the Dutch
poet Hadewijch.

ADRICHONIA, CORNELIA: sixteenth century, Nether-
lands.
Work: a poetical version of Psalms and other
religious poetry.
She was a nun of the Saint Augustine order.

AFRA, APHARA, AYFARA: various spellings for
Aphra Behn.

AGNEW: maiden name of Margaret Blennerhassett.

AHMEDI: family name of Aisha.

AIKIN: maiden name of Mary E. Brooks and Anna
Letitia Barbauld.

AIKIN, LUCY: 1781-1864, England. a.k.a. Mary
Godolphin.
Work: poetry, histories, memoirs, biograp-
hies, letters; *Epistles on Women*, 1810.
She was a lively talker and letter writer;
her work reflects the religious, philoso-
phical and literary climate of her circle.

AISHA: twelfth century, Cordova, Spain. Family
name, Ahmedi.
Work: poems.
Her poems and orations were read with ap-
plause in the Royal Academy of Cordova.

ALAIS: fl. 1150-1250, Provence, France.
Work: found in *The Women Troubadours*, pp.
144-5 and 178-9.

ALAMANDA: fl. second half twelfth century, Gas-
con, France.
Work: found in *The Women Troubadours*, pp.
102-7 and 170.

ALARCON: see Cristobalina Fernandez de Alarcon,
under F.

ALBEDYHL, BARONESS D': fl. 1814, Sweden. a.k.a.
The Swedich Sevigne.

Work: *Gefion,* an epic poem, 1814, Upsala.
ALBRET, JEANNE D': 1528-1572; Navarre, France.
    Work: poetry and prose.
    Like her mother, Margaret of Navarre, 1492-
    1549, she was a patron of the Reformation
    in France.
ALDERSON: maiden name of Amelia Opie.
ALENCON: first married name of Margaret of
    Navarre, 1492-1549.
ALFARSULI: see Maria Abi Jacobi Alfarsuli,
    under M.
AL-KHANSA or HANSA: listed under K.
ALMEIDA: see Leonor de Alorna.
ALMODIS OF CASENEUVE: see next entry.
ALMUCS DE CASTELNAU: a.k.a. Almodis of Caseneuve;
    c. 1140; Provence, France.
    Work: found in *The Woman Troubadours,* pp.
    92-3 and 165.
    She was a patron of troubadours.
ALORNA, LEONOR ALMEIDA PORTUGAL LORENA Y LAN-
    CASTER, MARQUESA DE: 1750-1839; Lisbon,
    Portugal.
    Work: *Obras Completas,* six volumes, 1844,
    Lisbon. *Ineditos: Cartas E Outras Escritos,*
    1941, edited by H. Cidade. *Poesias,* 1941,
    edited by H. Cidade.
    She exercised considerable influence on the
    Romantic generation in Portugal by her origi-
    nal compositions and translations from early
    English and French Romantics. She inherited
    her title, De Alorna, from her brother on his
    death.
ALPHAIZULI, MARIA: eighth century, Seville,
    Spain. a.k.a. Arabian Sappho.
    Work: poetry in the library of the Escurial.
    She may be the same poet as Maria Abi Jacobi
    Alfarsuli and Maria de Hispali, both under M.
ALTOVITI, MARSEILLE D': died 1609; Florence,
    Italy.
    Work: poems.
    She settled at Marseille and devoted herself
    to writing Italian poetry.
AMALTHEA: see Sibyl of Cumai.

AMARILIS: real name unknown: seventeenth cen-
    tury; Spanish America.
    Work: poems found in Lope de Vega's *Filo-
    mena*, 1621.
    Quite a few women have been mentioned as pos-
    sible identities for Amarilis: Marta de Nev-
    ares Santoyo, Maria de Alvarado, Isabelle
    Figueroa, Maria Rojas y Gavoy, and Maria
    Tello de Sotomayor.
AMARILLI ETRUSCA: name of Teresa Bandettini, in
    the Arcadia Academia.
AMERICAN HEMANS: popular name for Lydia Sigourney.
AMERICAN MONTAGUE: popular name for Sarah Morton.
AMERICAN SAPPHO: another popular name for Sarah
    Morton.
AMIS: sometimes thought to be the maiden name of
    Aphra Behn.
AMMANATI, LAURA BATTIFERRI: 1523-1589; Florence,
    Italy. a.k.a. Second Sappho.
    Work: religious poems.
    She was a member of the Introvati Academy at
    Sienna.
ANDAL: fl. 800, India.
    Work: found in *Hymns of the Alvars*, 1932;
    and *Hymns of Tamil Savite Saints*, 1921. She
    is one of twelve Tamil poet-saints whose
    hymns are used in Vaishnana temples in south-
    ern India.
ANDREINI, ISABELLA: 1562-1604; Padua, Italy.
    a.k.a. Comica Gelosa.
    Work: *Aeterna Fama*.
    She was an actress; spoke French and Span-
    ish; knew philosophy, sciences, poetry; she
    was a member of the Academia Intenta of Pa-
    via; had seven children, and was a leading
    lady of the Gelosi company.
ANDUZA, CLARA D': a.k.a. Andusa, Clara D'; fl.
    first half thirteenth century, Provence,
    France.
    Work: found in *The Women Troubadours*, pp.
    130 and 176.
    She was probably the wife or daughter of
    the Lord of Anduze, one of the most impor-

tant towns in Languedoc.

ANGOULEME: the family name of Margaret of Navarre.

ANNA MATILDA: pseudonym of Hannah Cowley.

ANNE GRANT OF LOGGAN or LAGGAN: pen name of Anne Grant.

ANONYMOUS: most of the women contained in the Index originally published their work either anonymously or under fictitious names. Therefore, it is essential to know their maiden names, married names, aristocratic titles, nicknames, pseudonyms and titles of their books for further research.

ANSPACH, MARGRAVINE OF: title of Elizabeth Berkeley, Lady Craven.

ANYTE: fourth century, B.C.; Tegea, Greece. Feminine Home.
Work: 20 epigrams in the *Greek Anthology*. Her poetry was so highly esteemed that in the famous Garland of Meleager the *Lilies of Anyte* are the first poems to be entwined in the Wreath of the Poets; her love and interest in animals mark her as typical of the early Hellenistic Period.

APTHORPE: maiden name of Sarah Morton.

ARABIAN SAPPHO: popular name for Maria Alphaizuli.

ARAGONA, TULLIA D': 1508-1556; Rome, Venice and Florence, Italy. a.k.a. Thalia and Synberrie, by Muzio.
Work: *Rime*, 1547; *Dialogo Dell Infinita D'Amore*, 1547.
She was a famous Hetaira; wrote of feigned ardor and simulated jealousies which show a Platonic philosophy of love; she contributed to the genre of romantic epic with her narrative poem, *Meshino Altramerte Detto Il Guerrino*.

ARBLAY, MADAME D': married name of Frances Burney.

ARCHINTA, MARGHERITA: sixteenth century; Milan, Italy.
Work: lyric poetry and music.
She was of noble birth, distinguished for

her talent.

ARDELIA: name used by Anne Finch within her
    literary circle.

ARISTODAMA OF SMYRNA: fourth century, B.C.;
    Greece.
    Work: poems.
    She gave recitals of her poetry throughout
    Greece and received many honors.

ARNOLD: maiden name of Catharine Williams.

ARUNDEL, DUCHESS OF: title of Anne Howard.

ASBAJE: family name of Juana Ines de la Cruz;
    under C.

ASKEW, ANNE: 1520-1546; Lincolnshire, England.
    Work: *The Ballad which Anne Askew Made and
    Sang when She Was in Newgate.*
    She was burned at the stake for refusing to
    reveal names of Protestant "heretics"; she
    was highly educated, devoted to Biblical
    study; felt herself superior to the clergy
    in theology. After her tortures and trials
    her self assurance was stronger than ever.

ASTREA: pseudonym of Aphra Behn.

ATHENAIS: original name of Eudocia.

AUBESPINE, MAGDALEN de L': a.k.a. her married
    name, de Neuville; died 1596; France.
    Work: poetry, prose and translations.

AUGUSTA: title of Eudocia.

AUTREMONT, D': first married name of Marie Anne
    Viot.

AVA: real name unknown; fl. 1130, Melk-on-Dan-
    ube, Germany.
    Work: 2,500 lines on Christ, anti-Christ,
    and the last Judgement. *Johannes der Taufer;
    Das Leben Jesu; Von den Sieben Goven des
    Heilige Geistes; Der Antichrist* and *Das
    Jungste Gericht.*
    She was the earliest German woman to write
    poetry in the vernacular who was known by
    name; she lived as a recluse near the monas-
    tery of Melk-on-Danube; had two sons before
    taking the veil.

AVIS: see Philipa of Avis and Lancaster, under
    P.

AVOGADRO, LUCIA: died 1568, Italy.
 Work: a few lyrics extant.
AZALAIS DE PORCAIRAGES: c. 1140; Provence, France.
 Work: found in *The Woman Troubadours*, pp. 94-5
 and 166.
 She was from the modern town of Portiragnes;
 she appears to have moved in courtly society;
 a noble and accomplished woman.
AZZI DE FORTI, FAUSTINA: died 1724; Arezzo,
 Italy. a.k.a. Eurinomia.
 Work: published a volume of poems. She was
 a member of the Arcadia Academia.

BABOIS, VICTOIRE: 1759-1839; Versailles, France.
 Work: poetry and prose.
 Though she was uneducated, her poetry was
 nevertheless popular in France.
BAILLIE: maiden name of Jane Welsh Carlyle.
BAILLIE, GRIZEL or GRISEL or GRISELL,LADY, (nee
 HUME or HOME): 1665-1746; Berwickshire, Scot-
 land.
 Work: poems and prose.
 At the age of twelve, she became a spy for
 her father and others in defiance of James,
 Duke of York; her family fled to Holland
 until the Restoration. She also wrote *The
 Household Book of Lady Grisell Baillie*, 1692-
 1733, reprinted in 1911; she was married
 for fourty-six years.
BAILLIE, JOANNA: 1762-1851; Bothwell and London,
 England.
 Work: *Fugitive Verses*, 1790; *Metrical Le-
 gends*, 1821; *Dramatic and Poetical Works*,
 1851.
 She had written only a few poems at the age
 of 36, when she began to write *Plays on the
 Passions* which were soon published anony-
 mously and created a literary furor; she
 had a salon.
BAILLIE, MARIANNE (nee WATHEN): 1795?-1830;
 Kingsbury, Twickenham, Devonshire, London,

England and Portugal.
Work: *Guy of Warwick, a Legende & Other Poems*, 1817, Kingsbury, privately printed; second edition with more poems, 1818; *Trifles in Verse*, 1825, London; *Farewell to Twickenham*, 1819, verse.
Essays and letters she wrote while travelling on the continent and living two and a half years in Portugal were also published.
BANDETTINI, TERESA: fl. 1794; Lucca, Italy.
a.k.a. Amarilli Etrusca.
Work: *Ode Tre*, Three Odes. *Saggio di Versi Estemporanci.*
An actress turned poet, she also translated from Latin and Greek to Italian; she was a member of the Arcadia Academia.
BARBAULD, ANNA LETITIA nee AIKIN: 1743-1825; Leicestershire, England.
Work: *Poems*, 1773; *Hymns in Prose for Children*; *The Female Speaker*, 1811; *Eighteen Hundred & Eleven*, 1811, a patriotic poem.
She was a member of the Bluestockings; from the age of two she fought her father for the right to be educated but still opposed formal education for women; she and her husband had a successful school for boys;she edited a 50 volume series on British novelists, 1810.
BARBE DE VERRUE: thirteenth century; France.
a.k.a. Troubadouresse.
Work: *The Gallic Orpheos or Angelinde and Cyndorix*, poem.
She travelled through towns and cities singing her own verses, and familiar ones like *Griseldis* and *Ancassin & Nicolette.* She acquired a considerable fortune in this way.
BARBER, MARY: 1690?-1757; Ireland and England.
Called Sapphira by Swift.
Work: *Poems on Several Occasions*, 1734, 1735 and 1736.
She had several children and began writing

8

poetry to enliven their lessons; though she suffered from gout she had to support her husband and daughters.

BARBIER, MARY ANN: died 1745; Orleans and Paris, France.

Work: tragedies, operas, and plays containing verse.

Sarah Josepha Hale says of her work, "In endeavoring to render the heroines of her plays generous and noble, she degrades all her heroes. We perceive the weakness of a timid pencil, which, incapable of painting objects in large, strives to exaggerate the virtues of her sex..." p. 203, *Woman's Record*.

BARKER, JANE: last half of seventeenth century; England.

Work: *Poetical Recreations*, 1688; *Love Intrigues, or the History of the Amours of Bosvit and Galesia as Related to Lucasia in Saint Germanis Garden, A Novel Written by a Young Lady*, 1713; *The Christian Pilgrimage*, 1718.

BARNARD, ANNE (nee LINDSAY): 1750-1825; Scotland and South Africa.

Work: poetry and letters.

She lived at the Cape of Good Hope from 1797-1802. Her house in London was a literary center. She mysteriously would not acknowledge authorship of her famous poem *Auld Robin Gray* until two years before her death.

BARNES: see Julians Berners.

BARONI, ADRIANNE BASILE: fl. 1639; Mantua, Italy.

Work: poetry. She was celebrated for her beauty, wit and accomplishments in a collection of poems in Latin, Greek, Spanish, Italian and French published in 1639.

BASILE: maiden name of Adrianne Baroni.

BATHORY or BATHORI, ELIZABETH DE, COUNTESS: 1556-1611, Hungary.

Work: *A Letter of Elizabeth de Bathory,*

freely translated into a poem by Anca
Vrbovska, in English, p. 15, from *From
Deborah and Sappho to the Present.*
BATTIFERRI: maiden name of Laura Ammanati.
B.B.: one of the pseudonyms of Caroline Nairne.
BEATRITZ DE DIA or BEATRICE, COUNTESS OF DIE:
fl. 1140-1160; Provence, France.
Work: five ardent love songs, addressed to
the poet Raimbout d'Aurenga, survive.
There is no satisfactory identification of
her; Die is north of Montelimar; there were
a dozen Raimbauts of Orange in the twelfth
and thirteenth centuries. That her name
was Beatrice is also questioned.
BEAUHARNAIS: maiden name of Hortense Bonaparte,
under H.
BEAUHARNAIS, FANNY COUNTESS DE: 1738-1813; Pa-
ris, France.
Work: poems, romances, a comedy.
Her essay *A Tous les Penseurs Salut* in de-
fence of female authorship was considered a
strange audacity though women of France in-
fluenced everything from state affairs to
fashions.
BECTOR, CLAUDE DE: died 1547; France. a.k.a.
Scholastica.
Work: wrote Latin and French poems, let-
ters, treatises. An abbess of St. Honore
de Tarascon, she was famous for her know-
ledge of Latin and her fine style of writ-
ing.
BEDACIEN or CATHERINE DURAND: early 1700's.
She married a Bedacien, but kept her own
name because she had begun to write under
it.
BEDFORD, COUNTESS OF: title of Lucy Harington.
BEE, THE: popular name for ERINNA.
BEECHER, ESTHER CATHERINE: 1800-1878; New York
and Connecticut.
Work: occasional poems, educator.
She opened a school for girls in 1823
with her sister Mary, which later became
the Hartford Female Seminary; though she

was an ardent supporter of education for
women, she opposed women's suffrage. She
stressed the scientific basis for the study
of home economics; she was possibly the
first woman to introduce physical education
into American schools for girls.

BEHN, APHRA (AFRA, APHARA, AYFARA) (nee JOHN-
SON OR AMIS): 1640-1689; England, Surinam
and Holland. a.k.a. Astrea.
Work: *Poems upon Several Occasions*, 1684.
Eighteen plays, twelve novels, the most
famous being *Oroonoko*, 1688.
The first english woman to support herself
by writing. She went to debtors prison be-
cause the government would not pay for her
work as a spy in Holland. She had to write
"like a man" in order to succeed; her ri-
bald plays earned her money and fame (in-
fame); her novel *Oroonoko* is a literary
masterpiece both for its early novel form
and the first treatment of sympathy for
black slaves. She thought of herself pri-
marily as a poet, but didn't have time to
develp this talent; nevertheless, it is her
poetry that is most likely to be found in
local libraries, in anthologies of English
poetry. A pioneer feminist, she claimed
the right to live her own life; she spoke
for sexual equality and openness in love;
she wrote of both lesbianism and male im-
potence.

BEL NUMERO UNA: see Ricciarda Selvoggia.

BELLE ANGLAISE, LA: pet name for Mary Robin-
son by Marie Antoinette.

BELLE CORDIERE, LA: nickname for Louise Labe,
a.k.a. The Beautiful Ropemaker.

BENEVENTE, CONDESA DE: title of Antonia de
Mendoza.

BENGER, ELIZABETH OGILVY: 1778-1827, Somerset
and London, England.
Work: poems published anonymously in per-
iodicals; also, novels, translations, and
biographies of poets, Elizabeth Hamilton,

Ann Boleyn and Mary, Queen of Scots.
She educated herself by reading books
through shop windows; her father sent her
to a boys school when she was twelve to
learn Latin. Left in poverty at her fat-
her's death, she moved to London where she
became friends with Mary Lamb, the Porter
sisters, Barbauld, Landon and Hamilton,
all of whom were poets.

BENITEZ, MARIA BIBIANA: 1783-1873; Puerto Rico.
Work: *La Ninfa de Puerto Rico*, The Puerto
Rican Nymph, 1832; *La Cruz del Morro*, The
Morro Cross, 1862; also decimas.
In spite of a meagre education she was the
first Puerto Rican woman to publish her
poetry and to write romantic lyricism; she
was blind the last ten years of her life.

BENTI-BULGARELLI, MARIANNA: fl. first half of
the eighteenth century; Italy. a.k.a. La
Romanina.
Work: poems.
She was a famous "cantratrice"; she helped
Metastasio who later became the Imperial
Poet.

BENTI-VOGLIO: the first married name of Bar-
bara Torelli-Strozzi.

BERGALLI, LUISA: fl. 1750, Italy. a.k.a. Ir-
minda Partenide in the Arcadia.
Work: poetry and theater management.
Inept at managing her household, infatuat-
ed with verse, she wasted her husband's
patrimony, then in 1758 she undertook the
management of a theater which failed, re-
ducing herself, her husband and five
children to poverty.

BERKELEY, ELIZABETH: 1750-1828; England. a.k.a.
Lady Craven, also Margravine of Anspach.
Work: poetry, plays, romances, memoirs, let-
ters.
Married in 1767, she had 7 children; separa-
ted from her husband 1781. She lived at
courts all over Europe; in 1791, she mar-
ried the Margrave of Anspach.

BERNARD, CATHARINE: died 1712, Rouen, France.
Work: verse, tragedies, romances.
She was a member of the Ricovrati Academia
in Padua.

BERNERS (BERNES, BARNES), JULIANS (JULIANA): fl.
early fifteenth century; England.
Work: a versified treatise on hunting in
the *Boke of Saint Albans*, first published
in 1486, recently reprinted 1944.
She was the first woman to write a book in
English; it was reprinted twenty times by
the end of the sixteenth century. She may
have been a prioress of the Nunnery of Sop-
well.

BERTANA, LUCIA: 1521-1567; Bologna, Italy.
Work: poetry, prose, music, painting, as-
trology.
She is Italy's third female poet, after
Colonna, and Gambara, of the sixteenth
century; medals were struck to her fame.

BERTHOLD, ERNST: pseudonym of Therese Albert-
ine Louise Robinson.

BERTKEN, SUSTER: c1427-c1514; Utrecht, Nether-
lands.
Work: poems and prose published in Leiden,
1518.
She was a mystic and poet who at thirty had
herself immured in a cell near Buurkerk.

BETJE and BETJE WOLFE: pseudonyms of Elisabeth
Wolff-Bekker.

BIERIS DE ROMANS: first half thirteenth cen-
tury; Provence, France.
Work: found in *The Woman Troubadours*, pp.
132-3, and 176.
Nothing known about her except her birth-
place; she wrote of love for another woman.

BIGNE, GRACE DE LA: died 1374; Bayeux, France.
Work: poems.
She accompanied King John to England after
the battle of Poictiers.

BIJNS (BYNS), ANNA: 1495-1575; Antwerp, Bel-
gium. a.k.a. Sappho of Brabant.
Work: poems published 1528, 1548, 1567;

reprinted 1949.

A school teacher for thirty-seven years,
she is credited with giving the Dutch lang-
uage its modern form through her writing;
before her time, it had been oscillating
between French and German.

BILDERJIK, KATHARINE WILHELMINA: died 1831;
Netherlands.

Work: poems.

She won a prize in 1816 offered at Ghent
for the best poem on the battle of Water-
loo.

BILLET: maiden name of Adelaide Gilberte Du-
fresnoy.

BINGEN, HILDEGARD OF: see Hildegardis.

BIRGITTA: popular name for the Swedish Saint
Bridget, 1304-1373.

BLACKFORD: maiden name of Mary Tighe.

BLAMIRE, SUSANNA: 1747-1794; Cardew Hall,
England. a.k.a. The Muse of Cumberland.

Work: *The Poetical Works of Miss Susanna
Blamire, the Muse of Cumberland*, 1842;
Edinburgh.

She began studying poetry by imitating her
favorite authors; all her poems were pub-
lished anonymously; she lived and collabor-
ated with Catherine Gilpin. Though she
lived in a rural area, she was a true poet,
catching the humor of the Cumbrian folk.

BLEEKER: maiden name of Margaretta Faugeres.

BLEEKER, ANN ELIZA (nee SCHUYLER): 1752-1783;
New York.

Work: *The Posthumous Works of Ann Eliza
Bleeker*, 1793; edited by her daughter, Mar-
garetta Faugeres, also a poet.

Married at seventeen, she lived at Pough-
keepsie and the frontier village of Albany.
Twice she had to escape for her life dur-
ing the Revolutionary War; her husband
was taken prisoner by the Tories; she lost
her baby, mother and sister within weeks
of each other due to malnutrition and hard-
ships of war. Somehow she managed to read

14

Homer, Virgil, Theocritus, Ariosto, and Tasso, and to write poetry. She died at thirty-one of a broken heart.

BLENNERHASSET, MARGARET (nee AGNEW): died 1842; Ireland, Ohio, Montreal.
Work: *The Widow of the Rock and Other Poems*, 1824; Montreal, signed "A Lady." She married in 1796, came to the U.S. that year; her home on an island in the Ohio River was headquarters for Aaron Burr; in 1805 her husband was arrested, and the estate ruined by the militia; she and her five children fled to Canada. Burr and her husband were found innocent in 1807, but the estate was ruined; she died before she was able to get compensation from Congress.

BLUESTOCKING: a term applied to a woman with literary tastes; it began about 1750 in London with a group of women meeting at the home of Mrs. Vesey. It was a substitute for card playing, then the principal recreation. The name "Bluestocking" refers to the color of men's socks, blue for everyday use, as opposed to the formal black silk. Hannah More's poem *Bas Bleu* is about the Bluestockings.

BOARDMAN: first married name of Sarah Judson.

BOCCAGE, MARIE ANNE (nee FIQUET, DU): 1710-1802; Rouen, France. a.k.a. Forma Venus Arte Minerva.
Work: *The Columbiad*, an epic poem; *The Amazons*, a tragedy. She was a member of the academies of Rome, Bologna, Padua, Lyons and Rouens; she was well travelled and famous for her beauty and poetry, thus the compliment, "A Venus for form, a Minerva for art." Her work was translated into English, Spanish, German and Italian.

BOEOTIAN SOW: name for Corinna by Pindar; she beat him five times in poetry contests.

BOGAN OF BOGAN, MRS.: pseudonym of Caroline

15

Nairne.

BOGART, ELIZABETH: 1806-18?? ; New York.
a.k.a. Estelle.
Work: poems published in magazines.
She began to write in 1825; her poems were
never collected, although there were enough
for several volumes.

BOIS DE LA PIERRE, LOUISE MARIE: 1663?-1730;
Normandy, France.
Work: poems.

BOLEYN or BULLEN, ANNE: 1507-1536; England.
Work: occasional poems.
Henry VIII's infatuation for Anne while
still married to Catherine, set off the
Protestant Reformation in England; after
their marriage Anne also failed to produce
a male heir (rather, Queen Elizabeth I),
was accused of adultery and beheaded.

BONAPARTE: see Hortense de Beauharnais Bona-
parte, under H.

BONNE DAME DE NOHANT, LA: nickname for Marie
Aurore Dudevant.

BORSH, MARIA: died 1773; Netherlands.
Work: collaborated with Aagje Dekken on
poetry.

BOTHAN: maiden name of Mary Howitt.

BOUDEWIJNS, KATHARINA: 1520-1603; Brussels,
Belgium.
Work: poetry published 1587; second edi-
tion 1603.
She wrote counter-reformation poetry in
lyric, dramatic forms.

BOURBON, ANNE LOUISE BENEDICTE DE: 1676-1753,
France. a.k.a. Duchesse du Maine.
Work: *Divertissements de Sceaux*, verse.
She had a salon at Sceaux, where she car-
ried on political intrigues under the mask
of pleasure, and devotion to literature;
her literary influence was nevertheless
more real and lasting than her political
powers. She had an excellent classical
education and a reputation for beating
her husband.

16

BOURDIC, DE: second married name of Marie Anne
     Viot.
BOURETTE, CHARLOTTE: 1714-1784; Paris, France.
     a.k.a. La Muse Limonadiere.
     Work: poetry, prose, comedy.
     She kept the cafe Allemand, thus her nick-
     name, "The Muse of Lemonade."
BOURGET, CLEMENCE DE: fl. 1550; Lyon, France.
     Work: poems.
     She was a friend of Louise Labe. It is
     said that she died of a broken heart at
     the loss of a lover.
BOUVIER: see Jeanne Marie Guyon.
BOWLES: maiden name and first literary name
     of Caroline Southey, who didn't marry until
     she was fifty-three.
BRABANTINE SAPPHO: nickname for Anna Bijns.
BRACHMAN, KAROLINE LOUISE: 1770-1822; Rachlitz,
     Germany. a.k.a. Louise.
     Work: *Poems,* 1800; Desau and Leipzig; *The
     Judgement of God,* five cantos, and *Blossoms
     of Romance,* 1816, Vienna.
     She suffered from melancholy; committed sui-
     cide by drowning.
BRADSTREET, ANNE (nee DUDLEY): 1612?-1672; Lin-
     colnshire, England and Massachusetts. a.k.a.
     The Tenth Muse, lately sprung up in America.
     Work: *The Tenth Muse, Lately Sprung up in
     America,* 1650, London. *Several Poems,* 1678,
     second edition with new poems, Boston.
     She is the first professional poet of the
     Americas; she came to the Massachusetts Bay
     Colony as a pioneer in 1630; had eight
     children; helped settle frontier towns; was
     the daughter of one governor and the wife
     of another; and wrote some seven thousand
     lines of poetry plus prose equal to that of
     any American of the seventeenth century.
BRAGELONGNE, AGNES DE PLANEY DE: twelfth cen-
     tury, France.
     Work: *Gabrielle de Vergy,* a versified ro-
     mance.
BRAMBATI, EMILIA: (married name Solza); no

date; Bergamo, Italy.
Work: poems.
BRAMBATI, ISOTTA: died 1586; Bergamo, Italy.
Work: poems published in Bergamo, 1587;
also, letters.
She was a classical scholar, understood all
spoken languages of Europe; she pleaded
several law suits by herself, without being
thought ridiculous.
BRAND, BARBARINA (nee OGLE): 1768-1854; Eng-
land. a.k.a. Lady Dacre, first married
Wilmot.
Work: *Dramas, Translations and Occasional
Poems*, 1821, privately printed; also, *Ina*,
1811; and *Pedaris*, 1811.
One of the most accomplished women of her
time, she was an excellent amateur artist
who excelled in modeling animals, espe-
cially horses.
BREGY, CHARLOTTE (nee SAUMAISE DE CHAZAN), COM-
TESSE DE: died 1693; Austria.
Work: letters and verses, published 1688.
She was a lady of honor to Queen Anne of
Austria; she wrote of metaphysical love,
and corresponded with Henrietta of Eng-
land and Christina of Sweden.
BREMER, FREDERIKA: 1801-1865; Finland and Swe-
den.
Work: poetry and novels.
A feminist, and protagonist of female eman-
cipation, she worked with much success and
self-sacrifice for social and political re-
form. Her stories have been translated in-
to almost all the languages of Europe;
eleven of her novels were translated into
English by Mary Howitt.
BRENNER, SOFIA ELISABETH (nee WEBER): 1659-
1730; Sweden.
Work: poems.
She is considered Sweden's first female
professional poet; well educated, she was
a linguist, and wrote in German and Latin
as well as Swedish.

BRENTANO, SOPHIA (nee SCHUBART): 1770-1806;
    Altenburg, Germany.
    Work: poetry and tales published in Ber-
    lin, 1800 and 1803.
BRERETON, JANE: 1685-1740; Flintshire, Eng-
    land. a.k.a. Melissa.
    Work: *Mrs. Jane Brereton's Poems*, 1744,
    with some letters.
    She was forced to live off relatives in
    Wales after her husband inherited and
    dissipated a fortune; her verse was pub-
    lished in *Gentleman's Magazine* and else-
    where; she had two daughters.
BREWS: maiden name of Margery (Margaret)
    Paston.
BREWSTER, MARTHA: fl. 1757; Connecticut.
    Work: *Poems on Divers Subjects*, 1757; in
    Connecticut, a second edition published
    1759, in Boston.
BRICHE, SOPHIE DE LA: 1730-1813; Paris,
    France. a.k.a. Countess D'Houdetot.
    Work: poems.
    She was a musician, as well as a poet.
BRIDGET ELIA: name for Mary Lamb by her bro-
    ther, Charles, in his essays for periodi-
    cals.
BRIDGET OF KILDARE, SAINT (BRIGID, BRIGIT,
    BREED, BRIDE): 453-523; Ulster, Ireland.
    a.k.a. The Mary of the Gael.
    Work: poem, *The Feast of Saint Brigid of
    Kildare*.
    She was the daughter of Brotsech, a con-
    cubine to Dubhthach; after a poor child-
    hood, she accepted Christianity and con-
    verted her mother; she was soon able to
    acquire their freedom by her faith. She
    received the veil with seven other vir-
    gins; founded the nunnery of Kildare, the
    first on Irish soil. The Convent of Kil-
    dare became one of the greatest monast-
    eries in Ireland, noted for the learning
    of its monks and nuns. She is a venerated
    saint, patron of Ireland after Saint Pa-

trick.

BRIDGET OF SWEDEN, SAINT (BRIGID, BIRGITTA):
1302-1373; Finstad and Wadstena. Married
name, Gudmarsson.
Work: *Revelations*, or Visions.
After eight children and a good marriage,
she entered a religious order; she found-
ed a convent for sixty nuns at Wadstena
and a separate house for priests; her ord-
er became a center of northern culture;
her followers were known as Bridgettines;
her visions dictated to confessors were
translated into Latin and read widely.
They contain powerful, poetic protests
against the wickedness of the papacy and
the Swedish crown of her time.

BRIDGETTINES: nickname for the followers of
Saint Bridget of Sweden.

BRIGID OF MUNSTER: popular name for Saint Ita
of Ireland.

BRISTOL MILKWOMAN: popular name for Anne
Yearsley.

BROOK, CHARLOTTE: 1740-1793; Ireland.
Work: *Reliques of Irish Poetry*, 1789; by
subscription. Contains old Irish poems
and one of her own, *An Irish Tale*.
A child of her father's old age, she was
educated by him; when he died, she became
poor; she devoted herself to the study and
collection of early Gaelic poetry.

BROOKE, FRANCES (nee MOORE): 1724-1789; Eng-
land and Canada. a.k.a. Mary Singleton.
Work: edited the *Old Maid*, a weekly, 1755-
1756, thirty-seven issues! *Virginia*, a
poetic tragedy, 1756, England; also novels
and translations published anonymously.
She married in 1756; they moved to Canada
where she continued to write successfully.

BROOKS, MARIA (nee GOWEN): 1795-1845; Massa-
chusetts. a.k.a. Maria del Occidente.
Work: *Judith Esther and Other Poems*, 1820,
by "A Lover of Fine Arts," *Zophiel, or the
Bride of Seven*, 1833, London; *Ode to the*

Departed, 1844, Cuba.
She researched extensively for exotic material for her poetry. She tried suicide twice, taking laudenum. Griswold was unable to bring out an edition of her poems.

BROOKS, MARY ELIZABETH (nee AIKIN): married 1828, New York. a.k.a. Norna.
Work: *The Rivals of Este and Other Poems*, 1829, in collaboration with her husband, whose pen name was "Florio."

BROWN: maiden name of Charlotte Elizabeth Tonna.

BROWN, ANNA (nee GORDON): 1747-1810; Falkland, Scotland.
Work: ballads which she learned from an aunt. She practiced reciting ballads as an oral art; her versions underwent change and development over the years.

BROWN, PHOEBE (nee HINSDALE): 1783-1861; New York, Connecticut, Massachusetts.
Work: poems found in various hymn books. Orphaned at eight by her mother, after losing her father when she was just a year old, she had a hard life. When older, she managed to escape household duties for a quiet spot for meditation; unkind interpretations of this habit led her to write *An Apology for my Twilight Rambles, Addressed to a Lady*, which included her best known hymn, *I Love to Steal Awhile Away*. She had four children.

BROWNE: maiden name of Felicia Dorothea Hemans.

BROWNELL: middle name of Anna Jameson.

BROWNING, ELIZABETH BARRETT: possibly the first major female poet. This Index ends with the birth of Elizabeth Barrett Browning for two reasons: there seems to be little research into early poets lives, whereas there is ample information and reprinting of nineteenth and twentieth century poets; also, Browning seems to be consistently included in major surveys of poetry, thereby marking some sort of advance for women in literature.

BRUN, FREDERIKA SOPHIA CHRISTIANA (nee MUNTER):
1765-1835; Graefentoma, Germany.
Work: patriotic songs of liberty.
BUDDHIST SISTERS: no date; India.
Work: Hymn, *A Psalm of the Early Buddhist
Sisters*, found in *The World's Great Reli-
gious Poetry*, 1923, compiled by Caroline
Miles Hill.
BUELL: maiden name of Sarah Josepha Hale.
BULGARELLI: listed as Benti-Bulgarelli, under
Benti.
BULLEN: another spelling for Anne Boleyn.
BURNEY, FRANCES (FANNY): 1752-1840; London, Eng-
land. Married name D'Arblay.
Work: poetry in her novels, letters, and a
blank verse play. *Diary and Letters, 1768-
1840*, printed 1904, six volumes.
She was considered a dunce, but educated
herself; at eight, she did not yet know the
alphabet; at ten, she began writing stories,
farces, tragedies, epic poems; at fifteen,
she burned all her work. Her first novel,
Evelina, was published anonymously when she
was twenty-five; it was an instant success.
She was asked to be Keeper of the Robes for
Queen Caroline, which has been described as
five years of "splendid slavery." After her
health failed, she left court, married at
fourty-two, and had a son. None of her la-
ter writing equalled the quality of *Evelina*.
BURRELL, SOPHIA (nee RAYMOND) LADY: 1750?-1802;
England. Second married name Clay.
Work: *Vers de Societe*, 1773-1782. Also, two
volumes of poetry published anonymously,
1793; and two tragedies.
She had two sons, two daughters in her first
marriage. Her tragedy *Theodora* was dedica-
ted to another poet, Georgiana Cavendish.
BYNS: another spelling for Anna Bijns.

CABOT: maiden name of Eliza Lee Follen.

CALAGE, DE PECH DE: fl. 1610-1643; Toulouse, France.
Work: poems.
She won the prize for poetry at the Floral Games of Toulouse several times.

CALLIOPE: muse of epic poetry in Greek mythology.

CAMPBELL, DOROTHEA PRIMROSE: fl. 1816; Shetland Islands, Scotland.
Work: poems published in 1816.

CANTARINI: maiden name of Clara (Chiara) Matraini.

CAPTAIN LAYS: name of Louise Labe when she served in the Army.

CARENZA: fl. 1150-1250; Provence, France.
Work: found in *The Woman Troubadours*, pp. 144-5 and 178-9.

CAREW (CAREY, CARY, CARYE), ELIZABETH, VISCOUNTESS OF FALKLAND (nee TANFIELD): 1585?-1639; England.
Work: *The Tragedie of Mariam the Faire Queen of Jewry*, 1613, London; also, a history of Edward II, 1680.
She taught herself to read French, Spanish, Italian, Latin, Transylvanian; she set up workshops in Dublin to train beggar children in trades; became a Catholic convert, was estranged from her husband, and lived in poverty the rest of her life.

CARLYLE, JANE WELSH (nee BAILLIE): 1801-1866; Haddington and London, England. a.k.a. The Flower of Haddington.
Work: poetry, letters.
Her verse was spirited, original; she was good at satire; sent to school at ten, she burned her doll, after the model of Dido; at fourteen, she wrote a tragedy. Her marriage to Thomas Carlyle was difficult, and her life often dull and empty.

CARMENTA OR CARMENTIS: ancient Rome. a.k.a. Nicostrata.
Work: poetry, music and agriculture.

She is credited with having changed fifteen
characters of the Greek alphabet to Roman
letters; thought to be the wife or mother
of Evander, and thus the prophetic mother
in the founding of Rome. Her name means
"the songstress"; it is possibly from her
name that poems were named "carmina" by the
Latins.

CARPIO DE SAN FELIZ, MARCELA DE (SISTER): 1605-
1688; Madrid, Spain.
Work: religious poetry.
She was one of the fourteen children born
to the two wives and several mistresses of
Lope de Vega; she was a nun of the Trini-
tarian Convent in Madrid.

CARROLL, MRS: first pen name, first married
name of Susanna Centlivre.

CARTER, ELIZABETH: 1717-1806; Kent, England.
a.k.a. Eliza.
Work: *Poems Upon Particular Occasions*,
1738; also, letters.
A scholar, she knew Italian, German, Spa-
nish, French, Arabic, and Portuguese; she
laid down a plan at the outset of her life
which she adhered to steadily to the end;
she never regretted not marrying. She
wrote three volumes of poetry; it was said
that her health was damaged by too much
study; she was a member of the Bluestock-
ings.

CARTESIENNE, LA: nickname of Mary Dupre, for
her knowledge of Cartesian philosophy.

CARVAJAL Y MENDOZA, LUISA DE: 1566-1614;
Spain and England.
Work: *Poesias Espirituales de la Vener-
able Dona Luisa de Carvajal y Mendoza.
Muestros de Su Ingenio y de Su Espiritu,*
Seville; 1885.
She became a nun at twenty-six; came to
London as a missionary in 1605; was twice
imprisoned. She founded a college in Bel-
gium for Jesuits.

CASTEL, DE: married name of Christine de Pisan.

CASTELLOZA: born c 1200; Provence, France.
Work: found in *The Women Troubadours*, pp.
118-9 and 175.
She was from Auvergne; one of the finest of
the women troubadours; three of her poems
survive.

CASTELNAU, HENRIETTE JULIE DE: 1670-1716; Brest,
France. Married name de Murat.
Work: poems, fairy tales, prose.
Her levity and love of pleasure gave her a
bad reputation; exiled to Auch, she was la-
ter recalled.

CASTIGLIONA: married name of Ippolita Tornella.

CASTILLO, LUCIANA DEL: seventeenth century,
Ubeda (Jaen), Spain.
Work: odes, sonnets.
In her youth, she liked music and poetry.

CASTILLO Y GUEVARA, MADRE FRANCISCA JOSEFA DEL:
1671-1742; Bogota, Colombia. a.k.a. Sor
Francisca Josefa de la Concepcion, and
La Madre Castillo.
Work: spiritual meditations, autobiography,
mystic poetry; her works were published in
Philadelphia, 1817.
She entered the Convent of the Poor Clares
while young, in her native city of Tumja;
was several times elected abbess; her model
was Saint Teresa, another poet.

CATELLAN, MARIE CLAIRE PRISCILLE MARGUERITE DE:
1662-1745; Narbonne and Toulouse, France.
Work: poems.
Her odes were popular and crowned by the
Toulouse Academy.

CATHERINE OF BOLOGNA, SAINT: 1413-1463; Bo-
logna, Italy.
Work: *Le Sette Arme Necessarie All Battag-
lia Spirituale*, (Revelation on the Seven
Spiritual Weapons); also poetry and other
prose.
She was maid of honor to Princess Margaret
of Este at the court of Ferrara; she joined
the Augustinian nuns in 1432; in 1457, she
was elected abbess of the house at Bologna;

she had the gift of prophecy and miracles;
was canonized in 1712.

CAUMENT: see Charlotte Rose de Caument de la
Force, under F.

CAVENDISH, GEORGIANA (DUCHESS OF DEVONSHIRE):
1757-1806; England.
Work: *Passage of the Mountain of Saint
Gothard*, 1802; other poetry.
A star of the aristocratic world, she was
a leader of more sensible clothing for wo-
men. She had three children, was politi-
cally active and a patron of the arts.

CAVENDISH, MARGARET (DUCHESS OF NEWCASTLE)(nee
LUCAS): 1623 or 4 - 1673 or 4; England
and France.
Work: poetry, 26 unperformed plays, es-
says, orations, philosophical discourses
and biography. *Poems and Fancies*, 1653,
1664; *Nature's Pictures Drawn by Fancy's
Pencil*, 1656.
She was well educated, a maid of honor to
Henrietta Maria; was afterward exiled with
the court to Paris and Rotterdam where she
lived in poverty. After sixteen years, she
returned to England to become one of the
first English women to publish her work;
she struggled to get her work accepted by
the universities, but was treated with
ridicule and disliked in court circles,
thus her nickname "Mad Madge."

CENTLIVRE, SUSANNA (nee FREEMAN): c 1670-1723;
Ireland and London. First married name
Carroll. First pen name, Mrs. Carroll.
Work: poetry, nineteen plays; and *The
Works of the Celebrated Mrs. Centlivre,
With an Account of her Life*, 1761-2,
three volumes.
A comic actress, she was compelled by ne-
cessity in her second widowhood to earn a
living; an ingenious writer of farce, she
anticipated the drawing room comedy of
Elizabeth Inchbald.

CEO (CEU), VIOLANTE DO: 1601-1693; Lisbon, Portugal.

Work: *Rimas Varias*, 1646, Rouen. *Parnaso,
Lusitano de Divinos, e Humanos Versos*, 1733;
Lisbon.

She became a Dominican nun in 1630; her
verse, both religious and secular, was pop-
ular in the seventeenth and eighteenth
centuries.

CERDA: see Bernarda de la Cerda Ferreira, under F.

CHAMBERLAINE: maiden name of Frances Sheridan.

CHANDLER, MARY: 1687-1745; Wiltshire and Bath,
England.

Work: *A Description of Bath*, poetry, third
edition 1736; eighth edition, 1767.

Brought up to business, she became a milli-
ner. She had a talent for poetry from
childhood, and studied diligently; she was
physically deformed; never married.

CHANG CH'UN-YING: end of thirteenth century,
China.

Work: found in *The Orchid Boat*, pp. 52 and
134.

She was a palace woman, part of a long tra-
dition of women captured in the wars between
China and Central Asia.

CHANG WEN-CHI: ninth century, China.

Work: found in *The Orchid Boat*, pp. 25 and
121.

She was the wife of an official, famous for
her short quatrains.

CHAO LUAN-LUAN: eighth century, Ch'ang An, China.

Work: found in *The Orchid Boat*, pp. 26 and
121.

She was a prostitute; her poems were a com-
mon type, sort of advertising copy in praise
of the parts of a woman's body, written for
courtesans and prostitutes.

CHAPONE (CHAMPONE), HESTER (nee MULSO): 1727-
1801; Northamptonshire, England.

Richardson called her "The Little Spitfire."

Work: *Miscellanies in Prose and Verse*, 1775;
The Works of Mrs. Chapone, 1807, Dublin, four
volumes.

She wrote a novel, *The Loves of Amoret and Melissa*, at the age of nine; her mother was jealous and suppressed her literary activity. Hester took over the household duties when her mother died, and continued her studies. She was a member of the Bluestockings.

CHARIXENA: Ancient Greece.
   Work: *Cromata*, prose and verse; mentioned by Aristophanes.

CHARLIEU (CHARLY): maiden name of Louise Labe.

CHARLOTTE ELIZABETH: pseudonym of Charlotte Elizabeth Tonna.

CHATTE, DE: second married name of Marie Catharine de Villedieu.

CHAZAN: see Charlotte Bregy.

CHENEVIX: maiden name of Melesina Trench.

CHEZY, WILHELMINA CHRISTIANE (nee VON KLENKE): 1783-1856; Berlin, Munich, Vienna and Paris. a.k.a. Helmina.
   Work: tales, romances in verse, operas set to music by Von Weber.
   Twice divorced, she was devoted to the education of her two sons; she was a granddaughter of the poet Anna Louise Karsch.

CH'IEN T'AO: early eleventh century; Sung, China.
   Work: found in *The Orchid Boat*, pp. 34 and 123; two poems survive.
   She was a concubine of a prime minister of Sung.

CHILD, LYDIA MARIA (nee FRANCIS): 1802-1880; Massachusetts. a.k.a. Philothea, a nickname given her by Lowell; also,The Female Franklin.
   Work: poetry, novels, essays, editing; she was an abolitionist and suffragist. *The Coronal*, 1831, poems; *Autumnal Leaves: Tales and Sketches in Prose and Rhyme*, 1857. She was in advance of her time; she was the first woman novelist in the United States; published the first periodical for children; wrote and published the first abolitionist volume in the United States, thereby losing

financial support. She was for women's
suffrage and pioneered in sex education;
held unorthodox religious views; she start-
ed a history of women which ruined her pub-
lisher; it was said, "Left to Lydia, doubt-
less this monumental task would have been
accomplished, but her publisher, a mere
man, went bankrupt at the fifth volume."

CHIYONI (CHIYOJO, KAGA NO CHIYO) :   pseudonym.
Her real name Fukuzoyo Chiyo; 1703-
1775; Japan.
Work: poetry found in anthologies of Jap-
anese Haiku.
A painter as well as a poet, she became
the most famous Japanese woman writer of
haiku, many of her poems reflecting sadness.

CHLORIS: nickname for Anne Wharton, by Waller.

CHRISTINE DE PISAN (PIZAN, PEZANO, PISA, PIZZANO):
1363?-1420?; Venice and Paris.   Married
name de Castel.
Work: poetry, ballads, treatises, bio-
graphies, autobiography.
An ardent feminist, she was the first woman
in Western Europe to earn a living by writ-
ing; she was the equal of any scholar in
the Greek and Latin languages.   Widowed at
twenty-five, with three children, she said,
"Alone I am, and alone I will be."   Her *Dit
de la Rose* was probably the first feminist
book written to protest the traditional
carping at women.   She was invited to the
courts of France and England.

CHU CHUNG-HSIEN (CHU MIAO-TUAN):   fifteenth cen-
tury; Chekiang Province, China.
Work: found in *The Orchid Boat*, pp. 55
and 122.
She was the daughter of a court official;
the wife of a country school official.

CHU MIAN-TUAN: see Chu Chung-Hsien, above.

CHU SHU-CHEN: early twelfth century, China.
Work: found in *The Orchid Boat*, pp. 45
and 122.
She was one of the three greatest female

29

poets of China; almost nothing is known of her life; her poems were published in 1182.

CHUDLEIGH: married name of Mary Lee.

CHUO WEN-CHUN: 179?-117 B.C.; Szechuan, China.
Work: found in *The Orchid Boat*, pp. 2 and 123.
The daughter of a wealthy man, she was widowed at seventeen; her subsequent love affair with a poor writer became a legend.

CICCI, MARIA LOUISA: 1760-1794; Pisa, Italy.
Work: *Poems*, published 1796.
She was sent to a convent at seven to be educated, but was forbidden to learn to write; she learned to read and write by stealth; read the best poets; wrote with grape juice and a pen of wood; her first verses were written when she was ten. She studied natural philosophy, English, French, the works of Locke and Newton.

CLARINDA: pseudonym, real name unknown: fl. 1608; Peru.
Work: *Discourse in Praise of Poetry* in tercets, 1608.

CLARISSA PACKARD: pen name of Caroline Howard Gilman.

CLAY: second married name of Sophia Burrell.

CLEOBULE or CLEOBULINE: 594 B.C.; Rhodes, Greece.
Work: riddles in verse.
She and her father were celebrated for skill in riddles; a well known riddle on the year is attributed to her.

CLEORA: pen name of Frances Thynne.

CLIFFORD, ANNE: possible identification of the Lady Diana Primrose.

CLIVE, CAROLINE (nee MEYSEY-WIGLEY): 1801-1873; Worcestershire, England. a.k.a. V, and Mrs. Archer Clive.
Work: *IX Poems by V*, 1840, several editions between 1840-1872; *Poems by V*, 1872, London. Also novels.
An invalid, she nevertheless married in 1840 and had two children. She was accidentally burned to death when her clothing caught

fire while she was bedridden, and sur-
rounded by books and papers.

COCKBURN, ALICIA (ALISON) (nee RUTHERFORD): 1713-
1794; Selkirkshire and Edinburgh.
Work: poems.
She was a leader of the social life of Edin-
burgh; she had original ideas of dress and
did not conform to prevailing fashions; she
wrote poetry all her life.

COCKBURN, CATHARINE (nee TROTTER): 1679-1749;
England.
Work: poetry, three tragedies and a comedy.
All her theater pieces were performed.
She began writing poetry at fourteen; her
first tragedy was produced when she was se-
venteen, in 1695, and published anonymously
in 1696. She also debated, and studied
philosophy.

COIGNARD, GABRIELLE DE: died 1594; Toulouse,
France.
Work: *Oeuvres Chretiennes*, 1595, religious
poetry.
She was the widow of a judge, Mansencal de
Miremont.

COLERIDGE, SARA: 1802-1852; Keswick, England.
Work: *Pretty Lessons in Verse for Children*,
1834; *Phantasmion*, 1837, a fairy tale with
lyrics; *Poems*, 1852.
She was a scholar and learned to read Greek,
Latin, French, German, Italian and Spanish.
The work of editing her father's (S.T. Col-
eridge) writings kept her from achieving
more in the literary world.

COLIGNY, HENRIETTA (COUNTESS DE LA SUZE): 1613-
1673; Paris. First married name Hamilton;
second, Suze.
Work: poems, songs, madrigals, odes; two
volumes, 1725. *Recueil la Suze-Pellisson*,
in collaberation with Pellisson, 1695; be-
came one of the most popular of seventeenth
century verse.
She bought off her second husband with twen-
ty-five thousand crowns for an annulment,

then devoted herself to poetry. All her
property was seized for debt, but she lived
well. A Protestant, it is said she became
a Roman Catholic so she would not meet her
husband in the next world! Her salon was a
sort of annex to the Hotel de Rambouillet,
the center of the "precieuse" movement.

COLLINS, ANNE: fl. 1653; England.
Work: *Divine Songs and Meditacions*, 1653,
signed "An. Collins."
In the prologue to this book, the author
says she has been ill; many of the poems
were written during her illnesses.

COLMAN: maiden name of Jane Turell.

COLONNA, VITTORIA (MARQUISE DE PESCARA): 1490-
1547; Marino and Rome, Italy.
Work: *Rime Spirituali* and *Canzoniere*,
religious poetry; also letters, published
in 1888. Betrothed at four or five, mar-
ried at 17 or 19, she loved her husband but
he loved the military; widowed at twenty-
five, she spent her life mourning him,
writing poetry, travelling from convent to
convent. Her religious poems, mystical in
nature, were so full of theological com-
plexities, so obscure and daring, as to be
frowned upon by ecclesiastic authorities.

COLVILL: married name of Elizabeth Melvill.

COMICA GELOSA: name of Isabella Andreini in the
Academia Intenta.

COMPIUTA DONZELLA, LA: the term for the Italian
poet, The Accomplished Maid.

CONCEPCION, DE LA: see Francisco Josefa del Cas-
tillo, under C.

CONSTANCE: see Marie Theis de Constance, under T.

CONSTANTIA: pseudonym of Sarah Wentworth Morton.

CONTARINI, GABRIELLO CATTERINA: end of fifteenth
century; Agolfio, Italy.
Work: *Life of St. Francesco*, a poem; *Life
of St. Waldo*, poem. Also occasional poems.

CONTESSA DE PROESSA, LA: pseudonym of Garsenda
de Forcalquier, under G.

COOKE: maiden name of Catharine Killigrew.

COPPOLI, ELENA or CECILIA: 1425-1500; Perugia,
Italy.
Work: Latin poems, *Ascetic Letters;* also
biographies and history.
She entered the religious house of Santa
Lucia at the age of twenty-seven; knew
Greek and Latin, and studied literature.
CORILLA OLYMPIA: name for Maria Maddalena Fer-
nandez in the Arcadia.
CORINNA: pseudonym of Elizabeth Thomas.
CORINNA (KORINNA, KORINA): late sixth century,
B.C. Tanagra or Thebes, Greece. Surnamed
The Fly; called Boeotian Sow by Pindar.
Work: poetry in Boeotian dialect; frag-
ments remain.
She is said to have gained the victory
over Pindar five times in poetry contests;
she wrote of heroines from Boeotian le-
gends; was a teacher of Pindar.
CORNELIA: pseudonym of Sarah Josepha Hale.
COSSON DE LA CRESSONNIERE, CHARLOTTE CATHARINE:
eighteenth century, Mezieres, France.
Work: poems published in periodicals.
COSTA, MARIA MARGARITA: born 1716; Rome, Italy.
Work: poetry published in Paris; librettos
of operas.
She was well educated; wrote in many genres.
COSTELLO, LOUISA STUART: 1799-1870; Sussex, Eng-
land and Boulogne, France.
Work: *The Maid of the Cypris Isle and Ot-
her Poems,* 1815; *Songs of a Stranger,* 1825.
Also essays and novels.
She supported her mother and brother by
painting miniatures; she educated her bro-
ther; never married, evidently by choice;
and she translated the works of others such
as Clemence Isaure.
COUTANCES: see Anne Marie Montgeroult de Coutan-
ces, under M.
COWLEY, HANNAH (nee PARKHOUSE): 1743-1809; Devon-
shire, England. a.k.a. Anna Matilda.
Work: two volumes of verse with Robert
Merry, 1788, signed by Anna Matilda and

33

Della Crusca; nine comedies, two tragedies,
two farces, and poems.
She kept a sharp eye on the production of
her plays, arguing vigorously with theater
managers over details, contributing to more
successful productions. She gave up writ-
ing plays in 1794, disgusted with the deca-
dent taste of London. Her comedies were
a among the first to be performed in the Uni-
ted States; "Anna Matilda" became a synonym
for foolishly sentimental writing.

CRAVEN: married name of Elizabeth Berkeley.

CRAWFORD, LOUISA McCARTNEY: 1790-1858; England.
Work: poems, several books of songs in col-
laboration with Professor F. Nicholls,
ECHOES FROM THE LAKES.

CRESSONNIERE: see Charlotte Cosson de la Cresson-
niere, as Cosson.

CRUZ, JUANA INES DE LA (SOR) (nee ASBAJE Y RAMI-
REZ DE SANTILLANA): 1651-1695; Mexico City,
Mexico. a.k.a. The Tenth Muse, Phoenix of
Mexico, and The Mexican Nun.
Work: *Inundacion Costalida*, 1689, Seville,
Spain; *Segundo Tomo de las Obras*,
Seville; *Fama y Obras Postumas*, 1700, Ma-
drid.
First major poet of Spanish America, she
was a precocious child; she learned to read
by stealth; begged to be sent to the Uni-
versity dressed as a boy; was sent instead
to an uncle with a large library. Her gen-
ius was recognized, and the Viceroy had
fourty scholars test her publicly; she be-
came a lady in waiting to the wife of the
Viceroy. At seventeen, she retired from
court to enter a convent; for the next twen-
ty five years, she studied, wrote poetry,
dramas, had a sort of a salon in her cell;
she had a library of four thousand volumes
and scientific instruments. At fourty-two,
she came under censure for criticising a
sermon by a priest; she sold all her be-
longings; died two years later in an epi-

demic while nursing the sick. Her *Reply to Sor Filotea* is a manifesto of the right of women to develop their minds.

CRUZ, MARIA DE LA: 1563-1638; Spain.

CULROSS, LADY: title of Elizabeth Melvill.

CUTHBERT: maiden name of Ann Knight.

DACRE: maiden name of Anne Howard, Duchess of Arundel. Also, title of Barbarina Brand.

DAIHAKU, PRINCESS: seventh century; Japan.
 Work: tanka (poems).

DAINI NO SAMMI: pseudonym of Fujiwara No Katako; 1000-c.1050; Japan.
 Work: *Sagoromo Monogatari*, a novel.
 She was the daughter of Murasaki Shikibu, also a poet; the daughter's novel is an imitation of Murasaki's *Genji Monogatari*.

DAMOPHILIA: c. 600 B.C.; Lesbos, Greece.
 Work: she composed a hymn on the worship of Pergaean Artemis.
 She is said to have been a rival or friend of Sappho's.

DAMSE SAPPHO: popular name for Sibylle Van Griethuysen.

DARBY: maiden name of Mary Robinson.

DAVIDSON, MARGARET (nee MILLER): 1787-1844; New York.
 Work: *Selections from the Writings of M.D.* 1843; edited by Catharine M. Sedgwick.
 Though she was bedridden for months at a time, seven of nine children died before her; she taught her children and encouraged their writing of poetry; she published the poetry of two of her daughters, both of whom died in their teens: Lucretia, born 1808, and Margaret, born in 1823.

DEBORAH: c. 1200 B.C., Israel.
 Work: *Then Sang Deborah and Barak (Upon the Rout of the Canaanites)*; from the Bible, Judges IV and V.
 She was a prophet and judge of Israel, who encouraged Barak to fight against Sisera,

and inspired the Israelis to win the bat-
tle; the nation had peace for forty years
under her rule.
DEBORAH: fl. early 1600s; Rome, Italy.
Work: poems; none extant.
She was famous while she lived for poetry
and other work; a Hebrew, her name may have
been a pseudonym.
DEFFAND, MARIE DE VICHY-CHAMROND DU: 1697-1780;
Paris.
Work: *Chanson, Les Deux Ages de L'Homme.*
Forced to marry at twenty-one, she spent
her early life at the court of the Duchess
du Maine (Anne Louise de Bourbon); she was
the center of a literary salon; was bril-
liant, witty, sarcastic; spent her last
thirty years blind and in a convent.
DEIPHOBE: see Sibyl of Cumai.
DEKKEN, AGATHE (AAGJI DEKEN):   1741-1804; Amster-
dam, Netherlands.
Work: patriotic and religious poems with
Maria Borsh; novels in collaboration with
Elizabeth Wolff-Bekker.
Orphaned at three, put in an asylum, she
made attempts at poetry; she was a comp-
anion of Borsh until 1773, then lived with
Wolff-Bekker; together they produced the
first Dutch domestic novels; they had to
write to support themselves.
DELANY, MARY (nee GRANVILLE):   first married name
Pendarves; 1700-1788; London and Bulstrode,
England.
Work: poetry; six volumes of letters pub-
lished.
At eighty, she began to write poetry after
a life of painting and drawing (flowers
were her speciality). Her first marriage
was forced when she was eighteen, her hus-
band sixty; her second marriage was happy;
she received a pension from King George III
and was a friend of aristocrats and Blue-
stockings.
DEMO & DEMOPHILE: other names for the Sibyl of

Cumai.

DESBORDES-VALMORE, MARCELINE: 1785-1859, Douai,
France.
Work: *Elegies and Romances*, 1842; *New Ele-
gies and Poems*; also, *Tears*; *Poor Flowers*;
Bouquets and Prayers; and *Poems of Child-
hood*.
Married in 1817, she spent the next twenty
years touring as an actress; had three child-
ren; lived in Paris after 1839. She support-
ed the family by doing hack work for publica-
tion; is considered one of the three most
important female poets of France, along with
Labe, and Deshoulieres.

DESCARTES, CATHARINE: 1635-1706; Rennes, France.
Work: an account of her uncle, Rene Descar-
tes, in prose and verse.
It was said of her that "the mind of the
great Descartes has fallen on a distaff."
She died of a disease brought on by "hard
study."

DESHOULIERES, ANTOINETTE DE LIGIER DE LA GARDE:
1638-1694; Paris. a.k.a. The Tenth Muse,
and the French Calliope.
Work: complete editions of her work were
published in 1695, 1747, and 1882; idylls,
eclogues, pastoral and religious poetry,
tragedy.
She studied Latin, Italian, geometry, philo-
sophy; she won a prize for poetry at the
French Academy; was elected a member of the
academies of Ricovrati at Padua and of Arles.
She had several children; was imprisoned at
one time because she insisted the King pay
her soldier/husband; was freed when he at-
tacked the chateau where she was being kept;
later, both were amnestied.

DESHOULIERES, ANTOINETTE THERESE: 1656-1718;
Paris, France.
Work: she published the poetry of her mother
(above) in 1695. Later editions included
some of the daughter's poems as well.

DESROCHES, CATHERINE: c. 1555-1587; Poitiers,

France (the daughter) and

DESROCHES, MADELEINE (nee NEVEU): 1530-1587; the
    mother.
    Work: three volumes of poetry, published
    jointly.
    The daughter excelled Madeleine in education;
    together they presided over a salon; Cather--
    ine would not marry because of attachment to
    her mother; in poetry, they expressed the wish
    not to survive one another; both died on the
    same day, of plague.

DEUTSCHE SAPPHO: popular name for Anna Luise
    Karsch.

DEVONSHIRE, DUCHESS OF: title of Georgiana Caven-
    dish.

DIE, COUNTESS OF: see Beatrice, Countess of Die,
    under B.

DINNIES, ANNA PEYRE (nee SHACKELFORD): 1805-
    1886; South Carolina, Louisiana, and Missouri.
    a.k.a. Moina.
    Work: *The Floral Year,* 1847; a collection of
    one hundred poems in twelve groups on flo-
    wers.
    Her poems were printed in Southern periodi-
    cals; she was married in 1830.

DIVINE SIBYL: another name for the poet, The
    Accomplished Maid.

DOETE DE TROYES: 1220-1265; Troyes, France.
    Work: poems.
    She was admired for her wit and beauty at
    Mayence, and attracted the notice of the Ger-
    man Emperor, but he found her virtue invin-
    cible.

DOLLEY MADISON: nickname for Dorothea Payne Madi-
    son.

DOMNA H: between 1150-1250; Provence, France.
    Work: found in *The Women Troubadours,* pp.
    138-9 and 178.
    Nothing is known about her; all sorts of
    suggestions have been made of names beginning
    with the letter H.

DOOLAEGH: maiden name of Maria Van Ackere, some-
    times Ackere-Doolaeghe.

DORSET, CATHERINE ANN (nee TURNER): 1750?-1817?;
Sussex, England.
Work: poems in her sister's book, *Conversa-
tions*, authored by Charlotte Smith; also *The
Lion's Masquerade*, 1807; *The Peacock at Home*,
1807.
Her mother died at her birth; she was raised
by an aunt; married in 1770, may have had at
least one son.
DOWAGER, THE: nickname for Dolley Madison.
DOYLEYS: maiden name of Katherine Dyer.
DROSTE-HULSHOFF, ANNETTE ELISABETH VON: 1797-
1848; Coblentz, Cologne, Meersburg, Bonn, and
Hülshoff, Germany.
Work: *Das Geistliche Jahr* (The Spiritual
Year), 1852; *Poems*, 1838; *Last Gifts*, 1860;
also novels.
Among the first of nineteenth century real-
ists in Germany, she is one of the best women
poets of modern times; she was not widely re-
cognized in her lifetime; she drew her inspi-
ration from nature.
DRUSBACKA, ELZBIETA (ELIZABETH) (nee KOWALSKA):
1695-1765: Poland.
Work: *Poezje*, two volumes, Leipzig, 1837;
religious poetry.
She was raised in the courts of nobility and
spent the last year in a convent.
DU BOCCAGE: see Marie Anne Du Boccage, under B.
DU GUILLET: see Pernette Du Guillet, under G.
DUDEVANT, MARIE AURORE AMANDINE LUCIE (nee DUPIN):
1804-1876; Nohant and Paris, France. a.k.a.
George Sand, and La Bonne Dame de Nohant.
Work: *Oeuvres Completes*, 1868, edited by M.
Levy, one hundred and five volumes.
Famous for her novels, letters, and autobio-
graphy this unconventional woman used a male
name, wore male clothing, smoked a pipe, and
followed her affections wherever they led;
toward the end of her life she lived quietly
on her ancestral estate at Nohant and compo-
sed pastoral poetry.
DUDLEY: maiden name of the sisters, Anne Brad-

street and Mercy Woodbridge.

DUFRESNOY (DUFRENOY) ADELAIDE-GILBERTE (nee BILLET): 1765-1825; Paris, France.
Work: *Elegies*, 1807; *Poesies Diverses*, 1821; also instructional works, vaudevilles, translations.
She married young, was ruined by the Revolution; Napoleon gave her a pension; she entered La Congregation Des Filles de la Croix.

DUMONT, MADAME (nee LUTEL): 18th century, Paris.
Work: published verse, fables, songs, and also translated Horace.

DUMONT, JULIA LOUISA: 1794-1857; Vevay, Indiana.
Work: *Life Sketches from Common Paths*, 1856; prose and verse.
She was one of the earliest women of the western United States whose writings have been preserved; she contributed to periodicals.

DUNGARVON: family name of Henrietta O 'Neil.

DUPIN: maiden name of Marie Aurore Dudevant.

DUPRE, MARY: 17th century; France. a.k.a. La Cartesienne.
Work: poems.
She studied Descartes philosophy so thoroughly, she was nicknamed La Cartesienne.

DURAND, CATHARINE: died 1736; France. She married a Bedacien.
Work: published romances, comedies, prose and verse.
She married a Bedacien but kept her own name, because she had begun to write under it; won a prize for poetry at the French Academy,1701.

DURBACH: maiden name of Anna Luise Karsch.

DYER, KATHERINE (nee DOYLEYS): fl. 1641; Bedfordshire, England.
Work: epitaphs on her husband's tombstone attributed to her.
The inscription on the tomb of the Dyers says they had seven children; four sons, three daughters; Lady Dyer is not conclusively the author; she may have commissioned the epitaphs.

EGERIA: name for Felicia Hemans, by Maria Jane
Jewsbury. Also the pen name of Sarah Helen
Whitman.

ELEANOR OF PROVENCE: died 1291; France and Eng-
land.
Work: she is reported to have composed an
heroic poem while still a child,in her native
tongue, possibly extant.
Married in 1236 to King Henry III of England,
she was very unpopular during the forty years
of her reign due to her awarding court posts
to relatives from the Continent who subse-
quently bilked the British treasury; had five
children; took the veil at Amesbury fifteen
years before her death.

ELIZA: pseudonym of Elizabeth Carter.

ELIZABETH OF YORK: 1466-1503; England.
Work: poems.
Grandmother of Queen Elizabeth I, her life
as exceedingly sad; she was caught in the
middle of court intrigues, and was a pawn in
royal marriages for political ends.

ELIZABETH, QUEEN OF ENGLAND: 1533-1603; London,
England. Family name: Tudor.
Work: *The Poems of Queen Elizabeth,* edited
by Leicester Bradner, 1964.
Better educated than any of the men of her
time, she excelled in Latin, Greek and French
before she was seventeen; she understood most
of the European languages; studied philoso-
phy, rhetoric, history, divinity, poetry and
music; her poetry was unpublished in her
lifetime; indeed, not published until 1964;
she wrote poems while in prison and on the
throne; her translation of Boethius in verse
is considered excellent.

ELLIOT, JANE OR JEAN: 1727-1805; Teviotdale and
Edinburgh, Scotland.
Work: one poem extant, "I've heard them
lilting at the ewe milking."
She lived in Edinburgh from 1782-1804; re-
turned to Teviotdale in her last year; it
is not known whether she wrote any other
poems.

ELLIOTT, CHARLOTTE: 1789-1871; Clapham, Brighton, Torquay, England.

Work: religious hymns, published as *Hymns for a Week; Hours of Sorrow,* 1840, and later editions; *Invalid's Hymn Book,* 1834, privately printed. She also edited the *Christian Remembrancer Pocket Book.*

In her youth she wrote humorous verse; an illness in 1821 left her a permanent invalid; in 1822, she gave up all secular pursuits; her hymn *Just as I Am* is still popular and has been translated into almost every living language.

EMBURY, EMMA CATHERINE (nee MANLEY): 1806-1863; New York. a.k.a. Ianthe.

Work: *Guido, and Other Poems,* 1828; *Love's Token Flowers,* 1846; and *Poems of Emma C. Embury,* 1869. She also wrote stories.

The leader of a salon, she never claimed authorship as a profession, but produced large quantities of poems, tales, and essays. She was an invalid the last fifteen years of her life.

ENGELBRETSDATTER, DOROTHE: 1634-1716; Norway.

She was the daughter of Engelbret Jorgenson.

Work: baroque religious verse.

She is generally thought to be one of the foremost hymnwriters of her day.

ENGLISH SAPPHO: popular name for Katherine Philips.

EPHELIA: pseudonym; real name unknown; fl. 1679, England.

Work: *Female Poems on Several Occasions,* 1679.

Joan Philips is one of the women suggested as writing under this pseudonym.

ERATO: from Greek mythology, the muse of love songs.

ERDMUTHE, SOPHIA (MARGRAVINE): 1644-1670; Baireuth, Germany.

Work: *The Christian Closet for the Heart,* hymns; also a treatise on history, published in 1666.

ERINNA I: fl. 610 B.C.; Lesbos or Rhodes or Teos
     or Telos, Greece. a.k.a. The Bee.
     Work: *The Distaff,* three hundred hexameter
     lines in Aeolic and Doric dialects; only four
     lines extant, titled "The Spindle." Also
     three epigrams of doubtful authorship.
     A friend of Sappho's, it was thought that
     her verses rivalled those of Homer; she died
     at nineteen, unmarried.
ERINNA II: c354 B. C.   Greece.
     Work: no poems extant. She celebrated Myro
     in her poems.
     She is mentioned by Eusebius and Pliny, but
     her very existence is questioned; often con-
     fused with the first Erinna.
ERNST BERTHOLD: pseudonym of Therese Robinson.
ESTANG, L': maiden name of Marie Anne Henriette
     Viot.
ESTELLE: pseudonym of Elizabeth Bogart.
EUDOCIA (EUDOXIA): 393-460; Athens, Greece and
     Jerusalem. originally known as Athenais, and
     later as Augusta.
     Work: a poetical paraphrase of the first
     eight books of the Bible; also of Daniel and
     Zachariah; canto verses of Homer applied to
     the life and miracles of Christ; a legend of
     St. Cyprian; a panegyric on Persian victor-
     ies of Theodosius.
     Carefully educated by her father, she was in-
     volved in the politics of her time; married
     Theodosius II in 421; in 438 went to Jerusa-
     lem on pilgrimage and returned in 443. She
     spent the rest of her life rebuilding the
     fortifications in a most formidable style;
     she also had churches built.
EURINOMIA: name for Faustina Azzi de Forti in
     the Arcadia Academia.
EUSEBIA: name for Frances Thynne in Dr. Watt's
     Miscellanies. Also a name given Maria Tes-
     selschade Visscher by Vondel.
EUTERPE: from Greek mythology, the muse of lyric
     poetry.
EX-QUEEN OF HOLLAND: see Hortense de Beauharnais

Bonaparte, under H.

FAEL, LA DAME DE (THE LADY OF FAYEL): thirteenth century, France.
Work: one poem extant.
Her poem is one of the very best of its kind; her lover was Chatelain de Coucy.

FAINI, DIAMANTE (nee MEDAGLIA): died 1770; Brescia, Italy.
Work: poems.
By fifteen, she knew ancient languages and had written several poems; she also studied philosophy, mathematics, theology and astronomy; she was a member of the academies of Padua and Rome.

FALCONIA: see Valeria Falconia Proba, under P.

FALKLAND, VISCOUNTESS: title of Elizabeth Carew (Carey, Cary).

FANE, ELIZABETH: fl. 1550; London, England.
Work: *Lady Elizabeth Fane's Twenty-one Psalms and One Hundred and Two Proverbs*, 1550, London.

FANSHAWE, CATHERINE MARIA: 1765-1834; Surrey, Richmond and London, England.
Work: *Memorials*, 1865; and *Literary Remains*, 1876.
A semi-invalid, she was nevertheless a gifted etcher and water color painter like her two sisters; her poems circulated in manuscript form or were published anonymously in the collections of others; her riddle on the letter *H* was often attributed to Byron.

FARNESE, FRANCESCA: died 1651; Rome, Italy.
a.k.a. Sister Francesca.
Work; poems in collaboration with her sister, Sister Isobella.
She founded a convent; wrote religious verse; out of a sense of duty, she burned a romance and poetry she had written before taking her vows.

FAUGERES, MARGARETTA VAN WYCKE (nee BLEEKER):

1771-1801; New York.

Work: *Essays in Prose and Verse*, 1795; *Belisarius*, 1795; a tragedy in blank verse.
Some of her poems are included in the works of her mother, Ann Eliza Bleeker. She was reduced to poverty by the wastefulness of her husband; she resorted to teaching to support herself when he died. She had one daughter. All three women, Grandmother Bleeker, Mother Faugeres, and daughter Mason, lived only thirty years.

FAYEL, THE LADY OF: see La Dame de Fael, under F.

FEDELE, CASSANDRA (MRS. MAPPELLI): c1465-1558, Venice, Padua, Italy, and Crete.
Work: a volume of Latin poems on various subjects; also letters and orations published in 1636 at Pavia.
She wrote equally well in three languages: Greek, Latin, and Italian verse and prose. She gave public lessons at Padua; was so prized by the Venetians that when Queen Isabella of Aragon invited her to court in 1488, the Senate refused to let her go to Spain on the grounds that Venice could not spare such a learned woman.

FELETTO: married name of Eleonora Ravira.

FELIZ: see Marcela de Carpio de San Feliz, under C.

FEMALE FRANKLIN: nickname for Lydia Maria Child.

FEMALE MILTON: nickname for Lydia Huntley Sigourney.

FEMININE HOMER: popular name for Anyte.

FERGUSON, ELIZABETH (nee GRAEME): 1737-1801; Philadelphia. a.k.a. Laura.
Work: *Hymns on the Charms of Creation*, 1766. Her poems, essays and letters were also published.
She was loyal to the Colonists, her husband to the British; they separated in 1775, and never lived together again. Her salon made a considerable contribution to the cultural life of Philadelphia.

FERNANDEZ, MARIA MADDALENA (nee MORELLI): 1740-
1800; Pistoja, Florence, Italy. a.k.a. Cor-
illa Olympia in the Arcadia Academia.
Work: published poems and letters.
She was tested for her poetic powers for
three days at Rome before a vast concourse
of literary and noble persons; the subjects
were philosophy, religion, physics, metaphy-
sics, heroic poetry, harmony and lyrics; she
then was crowned with a laurel wreath.
FERNANDEZ DE ALARCON, CRISTOBALINA: 1576-1646;
Antequera, Spain.
Work: quintillas on Saint Teresa, and other
poems; also romances, decimas, and sonnets.
FERREIRA, BERNARDA DE LA CERDA (FERREYRA): 1595-
1644; Lisbon, Portugal.
Work: *Liberated Spain*, a poetic history;
Lisbon, 1618 and 1673.
Well educated by her father, she also wrote
plays, sonnets, decimas, liras, comedies,
historical works, and dialogues.
FIDELMA PARTENIDE: name of Massini Petronella
Paolini in the Arcadia.
FINCH, ANNE, COUNTESS OF WINCHILSEA (nee KINGS-
MILL): 1661-1720; Sidmonton, England. a.k.a.
Ardelia within her literary circle.
Work: *Poems on Several Occasions*, 1713; re-
printed in 1903 and 1928.
She was maid of honor to Mary of Modena; she
wrote on love, nature, religion, plays, sat-
ires, parodies, as well as translations and
literary criticism. She often wrote about
women; was forced to become a poet in hiding;
she was often satirized in contemporary plays
because of her talent, but she remained mili-
tant in defense of her sex, bold in her crit-
icism of male poets and court life; her na-
ture poetry foreshadowed the Romantic move-
ment by a hundred years.
FIQUET: maiden name of Marie Anne du Boccage.
FIRST OF WOMEN: Johnson's name for Hester Thrale.
FLAGG: middle name of Hannah Gould.
FLAVIA: name for Anne Finch by Nicholas Rowe.

FLEMING: second married name of Ann Cuthbert
    Knight.
FLEMING, MARJORIE (MARGARET): 1803-1811; Kir-
    caldy, Scotland. a.k.a. Pet Marjorie, a
    nickname.
    WORK: *Complete Marjorie Fleming,* poems and
    diary.
    Though she died at eight of measles compli-
    cations, her poetry is still being printed
    in anthologies; she began writing verses at
    six; she was precocious but had a childlike
    personality. Her death was such a blow to
    her father that he never mentioned her name
    again.
FLETCHER: married name of Maria Jane Jewsbury.
FLORE DE ROSE: 1200s; France.
    Work: poems.
FLOWER: maiden name of Sarah Adams.
FLOWER OF HADDINGTON: popular name for Jane Car-
    lyle, in her youth.
FLOWER OF STRATHEARN: popular name for Caroline
    Nairne.
FLY, THE: surname of Corinna of Tanagra.
FOLLEN, ELIZA LEE (nee CABOT): 1787-1860; Massa-
    chusetts.
    Work: *A Well Spent Hour,* 1827; *Poems,* 1839;
    Anti-Slavery Hymns and Songs, 1855; also sto-
    ries and dramas.
    One of thirteen children, she was well educa-
    ted; married a man nine years younger; they
    had one child. She was active in the Sunday
    School movement, children's education, and
    anti-slavery; she had to write to support
    herself and her son after her husband's
    death; she also wrote on women's rights. Her
    mother also was of strong character and men-
    tal ability.
FONTE, MODERATA: pseudonym of Modesta Pazzo.
FORCALQUIER: see Garsenda de Forcalquier, under
    G.
FORCE, CHARLOTTE ROSE DE CAUMENT DE LA: 1654-
    1724, France.
    Work: *Castle in Spain,* a poem; also tales and

a romance.

FORMA VENUS ARTE MINERVA: descriptive name for Marie Anne du Boccage: A Venus for form, a Minerva for art.

FORTI: see Faustina Azzi de Forti, under A.

FOSTER: maiden name of Anna Maria Wells.

FOWLER: maiden name of Eliza Haywood, and Katharine Philips.

FRANCE: see Margaret of France, and Marie de France, both under M.

FRANCESCA, SISTER: see Francesca Farnese.

FRANCIS: maiden name of Lydia Maria Child.

FRANCO, VERONICA: 1546-1590; Venice, Italy.
Work: *Terze Rime*, 1575; Venice; other sonnets.
A courtesan and poet, she later gave up this life and devoted herself to good works; she established a society for the rehabilitation of prostitutes. Some of her poems are tinged with crude but realistic sensuality.

FRANKLIN, ELEANOR ANN (nee PORDEN): 1797-1825, England.
Work: *The Veils, or The Triumph of Constancy*, a poem in six books, 1815; also a short poem on the Arctic Expedition, 1818; and *Coeur de Lion, an Epic Poem in Sixteen Cantos*, 1822, two volumes.
Her first work was published when she was eighteen; the rest of her work was all published before she was twenty-five. She married at twenty-six, had a daughter at twenty-seven, and died at twenty-eight.

FRANZ, AGNES: born 1795; Silesia, Germany.
Work; poems published in 1826; *Parables*, 1829, Wesel; *Flowers that Pass*, 1833, Essen; and *Collected Works*, Breslau, reprinted 1833 in Essen.

FREEMAN: maiden name of Susanna Centlivre.

FRENCH CALLIOPE: nickname for Antoinette de Ligier de la Garde Deshoulieres.

FUJIWARA, LADY: 7th century, Japan.
Work: Tanka (poems).

FUJIWARA NO KATAKO: real name of Daini no Sammi.

FUKUZOYO CHIYO: real name of Chiyoni.
FULLER: middle name of Sarah Flower Adams.
FURIOUS SAPPHO: Pope's name for Mary Wortley
    Montague.

GABRIELLI: Maiden name or pseudonym of Mary
    Meeke.
GAETANS, AURORA: 1669-1730; Calabria, Italy.
    a.k.a. Lucinda Coritsea.
    Work: poems found in the collection of Ber-
    galli.
    She was a member of the Arcadia Academia.
GAILLARD, JANE: 16th century; Lyon, France.
    Work: poetry, none extant, only her name is
    recorded in a collection of Lyonese authors.
GAMBARA, VERONICA: 1485-1550; Brescia and Bolog-
    na, Italy.
    Work: *Rime*, 1759, Brescia; also letters.
    Though widowed young, she rejected all suit-
    ors; she was devoted to the education of her
    two sons and to literature; she wore black
    the rest of her life; wrote poetry as a lit-
    erary exercise, not out of necessity or ima-
    gination or emotion; she governed the city
    with good sense after the death of her hus-
    band, Gilberto, the Lord of Correggio.
GANDERSHEIM: see Hrotsvitha.
GARDE, DE LA: see Antoinette Deshoulieres.
GARSENDA, DE FORCALQUIER: c.1170; Provence,
    France. a.k.a. La Contessa de Proessa.
    Work: found in *The Women Troubadours*, pp.
    108-9, 170-1.
    She belonged by birth to one leading family
    of Provence, and by marriage to another; af-
    ter the death of her husband, Alphonse II,
    she ruled Provence from 1209 to 1217 or 1220,
    while living at Aix.
GAY: maiden name of Delphine Girardin.
GEORGE SAND: pseudonym of Marie Aurore Dudevant,
    under D.
GERMAN SAPPHO: nickname for Anna Luise Karsch.
GHIRADELLI, LAURA FELICE: fl. 1675; Bologna,

Italy.

Work: poems. One sonnet extant.

GILBERT: married name of Ann Taylor.

GILMAN, CAROLINE (nee HOWARD): 1794-1888; Bos-
ton, Washington, South Carolina. a.k.a. Mrs.
Clarissa Packard, her pen name.

Work: *Poetry of Travelling in the U.S.*, 1838;
edited *Oracles from the Poets*, 1844; *Verses of
a Lifetime*, 1849; and *Poems by Mother and
Daughter*, 1872, with her daughter.

She began writing poetry at eight, published
two poems by 1817; did not become professional
until 1830, when she was over thirty-six; she
had seven children; wrote domestics, romances,
tales, ballads and travel pieces; she was
firmly for the southern cause.

GILPIN, CATHERINE: fl. 1750; England.

Work: poetry in collaboration with Susanna
Blamire.

GIRARDIN, DELPHINE (nee GAY): 1804-1855; France.
Le Vicomte de Launay was her pen name in col-
laboration with her husband; a.k.a. La Muse
de la Patrie.

Work: *Poems*, 1827; 1833; 1857; also plays and
novels.

She was carefully educated by her celebrated
mother, Sophie Gay; she won fame for her poet-
ry by age fifteen, an academic prize at
eighteen, and a royal pension at twenty. She
innovated a highly successful weekly gossip
column in 1836-9; was admired by Classicists
and Romanticists alike.

GLORVINA: popular name for Sydney Owenson Morgan.

GONZAGA, COLONNA IPPOLITA: fl. 15th century,
Italy.

Work: a volume of poems extant.

She was educated, but her ten brothers were
not; her father believed men should know mili-
tary discipline, and morals would be developed
by long-suffering, while women should be
taught literature and science because their
domain was indoors. She died at twenty-eight
after two marriages.

ORDON: maiden name of Anna Brown.

ORE, CATHERINE GRACE FRANCES (nee MOODY): 1799-1861; Nottingham, England; and France.
Work: Seventy novels, which, with her poetry and plays, comprised two hundred volumes.
An army wife, she wrote many novels based on army high life; she was know to her childhood playmates as The Poetess; she married in 1823 and had ten children; her novels, published anonymously, were very popular; she also wrote music and songs.

OULD, HANNAH FLAGG: 1789-1865; Vermont and Massachusetts.
Work: *Poems*, 1832; *New Poems*, 1850; *The Golden Vase, Hymns and Poems for Children; The Youth's Coronal*; and lots more.
She was a popular poet for twenty years; she began writing in her mid-thirties; was her father's housekeeper and never married. She set her hometown laughing with her mock epitaphs on local celebrities.

OURNAY, DEMOISELLE DE: title of Marie de Jars, under J.

OWEN: maiden name of Maria Brooks.

RAEME: maiden name of Elizabeth Ferguson.

RAHAM, ISABELLA (nee MARSHALL): 1742-1814; Lanark, Scotland; Canada, Antigua and New York.
Work: *Life and Writings*, published both in England and the United States; also letters and poems.
She was an educator and philanthropist. Well educated, she turned to teaching young women in order to support her father, children and herself in Scotland after the death of her husband. In 1789, she emigrated to New York, where she again opened a school for young women; she founded the Widow's Society, the Orphan's Asylum, and the Society for the Promotion of Industry.

RAHAM, JANET: 1723-1805; Dumfrieshire and Edinburgh, Scotland.
Work: poem, *The Wayward Wife*, and other poems.

GRANDMOTHER OF BOSTON and GRANDMOTHER OF THE KIN-
DERGARTEN: nicknames of Elizabeth Palmer
Peabody.
GRANT, ANNE (nee MACVICAR): 1755-1838; Scotland
and New York. a.k.a. Anne Grant of Loggan
(or Laggan).
Work: *Poems*, 1802; *The Highlanders and
Other Poems*, 1808; also memoirs, letters and
essays. She came to America as a child, liv-
ed in Albany; returned to Scotland and mar-
ried in 1779; had eight children. When her
husband died in 1801, she had to resort to
writing for subsistence, as well as taking
in boarders; she also received a royal pen-
sion.
GRANVILLE: maiden name of Mary Delany.
GRAY, MRS. (nee LEWERS): 1800-?; United States,
native of Ireland.
Work: found in *The Female Poets of America*,
edited by Caroline May.
GREGORIA, FRANCISCA, SOR: 1653-1736; Seville,
Spain.
Work: poems.
Born of Flemish-Spanish parents, she entered
the Carmelite convent in Seville; rose to
eminence for her sanctity and mystical qual-
ities of her poetry.
GREVILLE, FRANCES (nee MACARTNEY): 172?-1789;
England. a.k.a. Fanny.
Work: *Maxims and Characters*, 1756.
She was the wife of Fulke; her daughter was
a Mrs. Crewe.
GREY, JANE: 1537-1554; England.
Work: one poem written on the wall of the
room where she was imprisoned in the Tower of
London, while awaiting execution for involve-
ment in court intrigues. She was seventeen.
GRIERSON, CONSTANTIA: 1706-1733; Kilkenny and
Dublin, Ireland.
Work: a poem found in Mary Barber's *Poems on
Several Occasions*, 1734; London.
Her parents were poor, illiterate country peo-
ple; she had little education; very few of

her writings were ever published; she studied Hebrew, Greek, Latin, French, and obstetrics; she also edited Latin classics, published by her husband.

GRIETHUYSEN, SIBYLLE VAN: 1620-?; Appnjedam, Groningen, Netherlands. a.k.a. Damse Sappho.
Work: religious poetry.

GRIFFITH: maiden name of Mary Pix.

GUDMARSSON: married name of Saint Bridget of Sweden, before taking the veil.

GUERIN, EUGENIE DE: 1805-1848; Chateau de Cayla, France.
Work: *Reliquae de Eugenie de Guerin,* 1855, Caen; *Journal et Fragments de Eugenie de Guerin,* 1862.
Her *Reliquae,* published after her death, went through sixteen editions in eight months. She was a lonely, melancholy, intensely emotional and religious woman; her love for her younger brother, whom she raised after her mother died, absorbed her life. She never married, and rarely left her domestic duties and good works; her conscience made her feel that time spent in writing was wasted.

GUEVARA: see Francisca Josefa del Castillo y Guevara, under C.

GUILLELMA DE ROSERS: fl. mid-13th century; Provence, France.
Work: found in *The Women Troubadours,* pp. 134-5, and 177-8.
She was probably from Rougiers, near Monaco.

GUILLET, PERNETTE DU: c. 1520-1545; Lyon, France.
Work: *Rhymes de Gentille et Vertueuse Dame de Pernette du Guillet, Lyonaise.*
She sang, played music, understood several languages; she wrote in Latin; she is one of three Lyonese poets who linked France with the poetry of the Italian Renaissance; she was the first representative in the French middle class of a literary woman.

GUNDERODE, CAROLINE (KAROLINE) VON: 1780-1806; Frankfurt-am-Main, Germany. a.k.a. Tian, her pseudonym.

Work: *Poems and Fancies; Poetic Fragments*.
She lived as an evangelical canoness at
Frankfurt; committed suicide for the love of
a scholar.

GUSTAVE: middle name of Ida Marie Hahn-Hahn.

GUYON, JEANNE MARIE BOUVIER DE LA MOTTE: 1648-
1717; France.

Work: *Cantiques Spirituels, ou D'Emblemes
Sur L'Amour Divin*, five volumes of commentar-
ies on the Bible; also letters.
She was sent to a convent at seven; at eight
was presented to the Queen, who requested her
services, but her father refused; married but
not happily; at twenty-eight, she was widow-
ed, with a daughter and two sons. She left
the children with relatives and travelled
from religious convent to convent; when she
died, the walls of her chamber, table, and
furniture were covered with verses. She in-
troduced Quietism into France; was imprison-
ed for her views for eight years.

HADEWIJCH: mid-13th century; Brabant, Nether-
lands. a.k.a Adelwip, in Germany.

Work: fourty-five spiritual love poems, six-
teen miscellaneous poems, fourteen visions,
and a number of letters.
She was among the first to produce spiritual
literature in the vernacular; the love poems
are in the style of Provencal courtly lyri-
cism; in Dutch medieval literature, her ta-
lent reaches a hight which has not been e-
qualled.

HAHN-HAHN, IDA MARIE LOUISE GUSTAVE (COUNTESS):
1805-1880; Mecklenburg-Schwerin, Mainz, Ger-
many.

Work: *Poems; New Poems; Venetian Nights*,
1835-37; also, novels, travel books and an
autobiography.
Unhappily married to her cousin, she was
divorced in 1829; she travelled to England,

Scandinavia, France, Spain, Italy, and the
East, publishing accounts of her travels.
She was converted to the church of Rome in
1850, became a nun in 1852 at Angiers, and
then devoted her life to aiding and reform-
ing outcast women in Metz.

HALE, SARAH JOSEPHA (nee BUELL): 1788-1879; New
Hampshire, Connecticut, and Massachusetts.
a.k.a. Cornelia, her pseudonym.
Work: *The Genius of Oblivion and Other Po-
ems*, 1828; *Poems for our Children*, 1830;
edited *The Ladies Wreath* and *Sketches of All
Distinguished Women from Creation to the Pre-
sent Day*, 1853; reprinted as *Women's Record*,
third edition, 1877.
Widowed at thirty-four, with five children
to support, she turned to writing. Educated
by her mother, she was a tireless proponent
of education for women; as the first female
editor of a magazine, she published women's
poetry and stories, and hired women to draw
fashion plates; she edited *Godey's Ladies
Book* from 1837-1877, breaking all previous
records, from 10,000 circulation to 150,000.
As a writer and editor, she influenced two
generations of women.

HALKET: maiden name of Elizabeth Wardlaw.

HALL, LOUISE JANE (nee PARK): 1802-1892, Massa-
chusetts.
Work: *Miriam*, a poem, 1830; *The Sheaves of
Love*, 1861; *Life of Elizabeth Carter*, 1838;
also poems in periodicals.
Married in 1840, she had at least one child.

HAMILTON: first married name of Henrietta Col-
igny.

HAMILTON, ELIZABETH: 1758-1816; Belfast, Ire-
land, and Edinburgh, Scotland.
Work: poems, letters, novels, essays, sket-
ches; *Memoirs, with a Selection from her
Correspondence and Other Unpublished Writing
of the Late Elizabeth Hamilton*, edited by
Miss. Benger, 1815.
Orphaned at nine, she was nevertheless well

educated by her relatives; she worked as a
governess, later received a government pen-
sion; titled herself Mrs. although she was
never married.

HAMILTON, JANET (nee THOMSON): 1795-1873; La-
narkshire, Scotland.
Work: *Poems and Songs*, 1863; *Ballads*, 1868.
Her parents were farm laborers, later shoe-
makers; she wrote numerous verses before she
was twenty on religious themes, but did not
write again until she was fifty-four, due to
having ten children. She was blind the last
eighteen years of her life.

HAN TS'UI - P'IN: 9th century; T'Ang, China.
Work: found in *The Orchid Boat*, pp. 24, 124.
She was a palace woman of the Emperor Hsuan
of T'Ang. It is said she wrote a poem on a
red leaf, which was found by a scholar who
later married her when she was released from
palace service.

HANNAH MORE OF AMERICA: nickname for Margaret
Mercer.

HANSA: see al-Khansa, under K.

HARINGTON, LUCY (COUNTESS BEDFORD, LADY RUSSELL):
1581-1627; England. a.k.a. Selena, by Dray-
ton.
Work: one poem survives, *Death be Not Proud*,
once attibuted to Donne.
She was a patron of poets; married in 1594,
she had no children.

HART: maiden name of the sisters Emma Willard,
and Almira Phelps.

HASTINGS, FLORA ELIZABETH (LADY): 1806-1839;
Ayrshire and London, England.
Work: original poems and translations publi-
shed in 1841 by her sister, Sophia Hastings.
Appointed Lady of the Bedchamber to the moth-
er of Queen Victoria, she lived at Buckingham
Palace until she died of a liver disease, ag-
gravated by court gossip that she was not ill,
but pregnant although unmarried.

HASWELL: maiden name of Susannah Rowson.

HATZLERIN, CLARA: fl. 1452-1476; Augsburg, Germany.

Work: edited a fifteenth century songbook of
Maeistergesang, including narrative, lyric,
didactic poetry, by both well-known and anon-
ymous writers.

She was a professional scribe, believed to
have been a nun; her edition of the Maeister-
gesang is the most important of the fifteenth
century, preserving the poetry of earlier wri-
ters.

HAUTPOUL, COMTESSE D': title of Anne Marie Mont-
geroult de Coutances, under M.

HAYDEN, ANNA TOMPSON: 1648-1720; Colonial Amer-
ica.

Work: mentioned as a poet by Harold S. Jantz
in *The First Century of New England Verse*,
New York, 1962.

HAYDEN, ESTHER: ? - 1758; Massachusetts.

Work: a sixty-seven line poem included in
*A Short Account of the Life, Death and Char-
acter of Esther Hayden, the Wife of Samuel
Hayden of Braintree*, 1759; Boston.

HAYWOOD, ELIZA (nee FOWLER): 1693?-1756; Eng-
land.

Work: *Poems on Several Occasions*, 1724; *Se-
cret Histories, Novels and Poems*, 1725; also
poems in periodicals, thirteen novels, and
four plays.

She married young, had two children and was
abandoned by her husband; she became an act-
ress, wrote plays which were produced; also
wrote thinly disguised court gossip.

HEDWIG, AMELIA VON (nee VON IMHOFF): 1776 - ?;
Weimar, Germany.

Work: *Legend of the Three Wise Men of the
East*, a romance in twelve cantos; also pa-
triotic songs and idylls.

At eight she could speak French and English
and write poetry; her romance was plagiar-
ized by male writers.

HEISEN: maiden name of Marguerite de la Sab-
liere.

HELEN: pen name of Sarah Helen Whitman.

HELFENSTEIN, ERNEST: pseudonym of Elizabeth Oakes Smith.

HELMINA: pseudonym of Wilhelmina Christiane von Chezy.

HEMANS, FELICIA DOROTHEA (nee BROWNE): 1793-1835; Liverpool and Wales. a.k.a. Egeria, by Maria Jane Jewsbury.
Work: *Works*, 1839; with memoir by her sister, Mrs. Hughes, seven volumes; *Poetical Works*, 1873 and 1914.
She wrote eighteen volumes of poetry, prose and plays, all popular at the time. She married at nineteen, had five sons; her husband left after six years, never to return. She was an invalid, fairly well educated by her mother; she could read six languages, and illustrated her own books; she was popular both in England and America.

HENSEL, LUISE: 1798-1876; Linun, Brandenburg, Paderbom, Germany.
Work: songs and religious poetry.

HERBERT, MARY (nee SIDNEY)(COUNTESS OF PEMBROKE): 1561-1621; Kent and Wales, England.
Work: *Psalms of David*, 44-150, with her brother Sir Philip who write numbers I through 43; *Lay of Clorinda*; she also revised Sidney's *Arcadia*.
She was a patron of literature; married in 1577; her version of the Psalms were not published until 1823, two hundred years after she wrote them; she is said to be the equal of her brother.

HERITIER DE VILLANDON, MARIE JEANNE L': 1664-1734; Paris, France.
Work: a novel in verse called *L'Anvare Puni*; tales in English; translations of sixteen of Ovid's *Epistles* in verse; other poetry.
She was a member of the academies of Jeux Floreau and the Ricovrati in Padua.

HEROPHILE: see Sibyl of Cumai.

HEYNS, MARIA: 1621 - ?; Netherlands.
Work: short stories with poetry, 1647.

HILDEGARDIS (HILDEGARD) OF BINGEN: 1098-1179;

Spanheim, Germany. a.k.a Sibyl of the Rhine.
Work: *Scivias*, prose account of her visions
in Latin; also homilies, prayers, hymns,
saint's lives, essays on recreation, redemp-
tion and duties of secular judges, medical
treatises and mystical interpretations of
nature, and poems in Latin.
She was abbess of the order of Saint Benedict;
although she learned to read, she could not
write; she dictated her work to a monk; her
book on medicine was considered the most
scientific of the time, a valuable record on
medieval knowledge of the natural sciences.
HINSDALE: maiden name of Phoebe Brown.
HISPALI: native city of the sisters, Maria and
Sophia de Hispali (modern Seville).
HO, LADY: 300 B.C.; China.
Work: found in *The Orchid Boat*, pp. 1, 124.
She was the wife of Han P'in who was arrest-
ed; she was then forced to marry the Duke of
Sung; she wrote a poem and hung herself.
HO SHUANG -CH'ING: 1712 - ?; Chiangsu Province,
China.
Work: found in *The Orchid Boat*, pp. 66-7,
and 124-5.
She came from a family of farmers, learned to
read and write from an uncle; she exchanged
her embroidery for books of poetry; at eight-
een, she married a farmer who was illiterate
and had a bad temper; her mother-in-law tor-
tured her.
HODSON, MARGARET (nee HOLFORD): 1778-1852; De-
vonshire, England.
Work: *Wallace, or the Fight of Falkirk: A
Metrical Romance,* 1809; *Poems,* 1811; *Mar-
garet of Anjou: a Poem in Ten Cantos,* 1816;
also translations, published in 1832.
Her mother was also a poet and writer; the
daughter married in 1826; she was a member
of Joanna Baillie's group.
HOFLAND, BARBARA (nee WREAKS): 1770-1844; Shef-
field and London, England. a.k.a. Hoole,
her first married name.

Work: seventy volumes of tales, novels and
poetry; also *The Life and Literary Remains
of Barbara Hofland*, 1849.
Raised by an aunt, she married in 1796; was
widowed and left destitute, wrote poetry to
support herself and her son, published 1805;
remarried in 1808, she helped support her
second husband with her popular novels.
HOHENHAUSER, PHILIPPINE AMALIE ELISE VON (nee
VON OCHS): 1789-1857; Waldau, Frankfurt-am-
Main, Germany.
Work: *Flowers of Spring*, 1817; also an auto-
biography and an historical play.
She married in 1809, was widowed in 1848.
HOLFORD: maiden name of Margaret Hodson.
HOLFORD, MARGARET (nee WRENCH): fl. 1778; Eng-
land.
Work: *Fanny and Selina, Gresford Vale and
Other Poems*, 1798; also comedies, tales and
novels.
She was the mother of Margaret Holford Hod-
son.
HOME: maiden name of Anne Hunter, and possibly
Grizel Baillie.
HOOFMAN, ELISABETH KOOLAART: 1664-1736, Nether-
lands.
Work: poems published 1729, 1734, 1744.
She had a difficult life, but wrote poetry
equal to that of her contemporaries.
HOOLE: first married name of Barbara Hofland.
HOPKINS: maiden name of Mary Pilkington.
HOPKINS, ANNE (nee YALE): 16?? - ?; Connecti-
cut.
Work: poetry and other books.
She was the wife of Edward H., Governor of
Connecticut. John Winthrop wrote that she
lost her "understanding and reason, which
had been growing upon her divers years, by
occasion of her giving herself wholly to
reading and writing, and had written many
books."
HORTENSE DE BEAUHARNAIS BONAPARTE, EX-QUEEN OF
HOLLAND: 1783-1847; Netherlands.

Work: occasional poems, music and romances.
She was the daughter of Josephine, and was
adopted by Napoleon after their marriage; she
married Louis Bonaparte, who was King of Hol-
land from 1806-1810; though separated from
her husband, her third son became Napoleon
the Third.

HOUDETOT, COUNTESS D': title of Sophie de la
Briche.

HOWARD: maiden name of Caroline Gilman.

HOWARD, ANNE (nee DACRE) (DUCHESS OF ARUNDEL):
1557-1630; England.
Work: an elegy written on the cover of a
letter.
Due to her influence, her husband became a
Roman Catholic in 1584; he was fined and im-
prisoned for life, and died in the tower of
London, 1595. She lived in poverty; the el-
egy is thought to be on the death of her
husband.

HOWARD, ANNE (VISCOUNTESS IRWIN): died 1760;
England. a.k.a. Douglas, her second mar-
ried name; Irwin was her first married name.
Work: her best known poem is a spirited re-
ply to Pope's "Characters of Women."

HOWARD, JANE: fl. late 16th century, England.
Work: poems.

HOWITT, MARY (nee BOTHAN): 1799-1888; England
and Rome.
Work: poems published 1822, 1827, 1831; she
wrote and collaborated on 110 works with her
husband William, including essays, history,
stories, translations, and articles on spi-
ritualism.
She was educated at home and in Quaker
Schools; she wrote verse at an early age;
married 1821; lived in Heidelberg and Italy
as well as in England; she was honored by the
literary academy of Stockholm for her trans-
lations of Frederika Bremer.

HROTSVITHA (ROSVITHA), HELENA VON ROSSEN: 935-
973; Gandersheim, Germany.
Work: *Comaedia Sacrea VI,* plays; poetic nar-

rative on the deeds of Otto the Great; elegies, and works published at Nurenberg, 1501. A nun of the Benedictine Order, she was Germany's first dramatist; she was also the first German female poet; she wrote in Latin, but the plays were German in content; her abbey was a center of literary activity.

HSI P'EI LAN: Ching Dynasty, China.
    Work: poetry.

HSUEH CH'IUNG: 8th or 9th century; China.
    Work: found in *The Orchid Boat*, pp. 23 and 125.

HSUEH T'AO: 768-831; Ch'ang An, Szechuan, China.
    Work: found in *The Orchid Boat*, pp. 21-22, and 125.
    She is the best known woman poet of the T'ang dynasty; she became well known when young, was honored at banquets and poetry contests given by the governor of Szechuan.

HUA JUI, LADY: 10th century; Szechuan, China.
    Work: found in *The Orchid Boat*, pp. 31-33, and 126.
    The wife of Jsu, the King of Szechuan, who adored her and called her Lady of the Hua Jui (flower pistil). When the king was defeated in battle, she was taken for the harem of the conqueror.

HUANG O: 1498-1569; China.
    Work: found in *The Orchid Boat*, pp. 57-62, 126.
    In 1519, she married a poet and dramatist; she was considered unique for her erotic poetry, usually not the province of women writers unless they were courtesans.

HUGGINS: maiden name of Louisa Caroline Tuthill.

HULL: maiden name of Sarah Judson.

HULSHOFF: see Annette Elisabeth von Droste-Hulshoff, under D.

HUME (or HOME): maiden name of Grizel Baillie.

HUNTER: second married name of Anne Seymour.

HUNTER, ANNE (nee HOME): 1742-1821; London, England. a.k.a. Mrs. John Hunter.
    Work: *Sports of the Genii*, 1797; with draw-

ings by Susan MacDonald. Also poems printed
in 1802; second edition 1803.
Known as a poet before marriage, she never-
theless used her husband's name as her signa-
ture; she had four children; was a Bluestock-
ing; Haydn set a number of her poems to mus-
ic.
HUNTLEY: maiden name of Lydia Sigourney.

IANTHE: pseudonym of Emma C. Embury.
IMHOFF, VON: maiden name of Amelia Von Hedwig.
IRMINDA PARTENIDE: name listed in the Arcadia
    Academia for Luisa Bergalli.
IRWIN, VISCOUNTESS: title of Anne Howard.
ISABELLA: c. 1180; Provence, France.
    Work: found in *The Women Troubadours*, pp.
    110-11 and 173.
    She may have been the daughter of a nobleman
    of one of the Christian empires of the East.
ISAURE, CLEMENCE (CLEMENZA): 1464-1499?; Tou-
    louse, France. a.k.a. The Sappho of Tou-
    louse, and The Queen of Poetry.
    Work: *Dictats de Dona Clamenza Isaure*, 1505;
    Toulouse; two copies extant.
    After the death of her lover, she entered a
    convent; before taking the veil, she turned
    her fortune over to the re-establishment of
    the Jeux Floreaux (Floral Games): poetry
    contests held on the first day of May. A
    bronze tablet in the Church of Notre Dame at
    Toulouse still remains, surmounted by her
    statue.
ISE, LADY: c. 935; Japan.
    Work: poems in anthologies of tanka.
ISELDA: ca. 1150-1250; Provence, France.
    Work: found in *The Women Troubadours*, pp.
    144-5 and 178-9.
ISEUT DE CAPIO: c. 1140; Provence, France.
    Work: found in *The Woman Troubadours*, pp.
    67, 92-3, and 166.
    She was probably from a small town in the
    valley of Luberon.

ISOBELLA, SISTER: fl. 1650's; Rome, Italy.
Work: collaborated in poetry with Francesca
Farnese.
ITA, SAINT (ITE, IDA, IDE, YTHA, IDEA, ITHA,
MIDE, MIDA, MEDEA) 480-570; Limerick, Ire-
land. a.k.a. The Brigid of the Munster.
Work: poems.
She refused to marry; after much opposition
from her family, she took the veil; founded
a nunnery of HY Conaill in Limerick.
IZUMI SHIKIBU: 974? - c. 1030; Japan. a.k.a. Oe
Shikibu: Izumi was her pseudonym.
Work: poetry found in a diary.
She was a court lady almost contemporary
with Murasaki; her family diary is mostly an
account of her various amorous affairs couch-
ed in a poetical style; she was regarded as
one of the best poets of her time.

JACOB, VON: maiden name of Therese Albertine
Louise Robinson.
JAMES: maiden name or middle name of Maria
Wales.
JAMESON, ANNA BROWNELL (nee MURPHY): 1794-1860;
Dublin, Ireland; Germany and Canada.
Work: *Diary of an Ennuyee*, 1826; *Character-
istics of Women: Moral, Poetical and Histor-
ical*, 1832; also memoirs, art, litarary cri-
ticism and poetry.
A miniaturist painter, she became a gover-
ness at sixteen; married in 1825; travelled
to Italy in 1846 to collect material for her
Sacred and Legendary Art, a storehouse of
delightful knowledge.
JARDINS, DES: maiden name and third married
name of Marie Catharine Hortense de Ville-
dieu.
JARS, MARIE DE (MARY): 1566-1645; Paris. a.k.a.
Demoiselle de Gournay.
Work: *Les Avis et les Presens de la Mlle.
de Gournai*, 1636.
She never married, received a pension from

the court; she was a feminist, a prolific
writer on morals and the defense of women.
JEWSBURY, MARIA JANE: 1800-1833?; England and
India. a.k.a. Fletcher, her married name.
Work: *Lays for Leisure Hours: Phantasma-
goria*, 1824, essays; and *Three Histories*,
1830, which includes a biography of Felicia
Hemans.
She said of herself, "Unfortunately I was
twenty-one before I became a reader, I be-
came a writer almost as soon." She was mar-
ried fourteen months before her death of
cholera in India.
JOHNSON: one of the two possible maiden names
for Aphra Behn, with Amis.
JORGENSON: family name of Dorothe Engelbrets-
datter.
JUDSON, SARAH (nee HULL):1803-1845; New Hamp-
shire and Burma. a.k.a. Boardman, her first
married name.
Work: poetry and translations into Burmese.
She was a missionary to India and Burma; lost
two children and her first husband on the
mission field; had eleven children, of whom
six survived; she was an expert in the Bur-
mese language though she was poorly educated;
translated *Pilgrim's Progress* into Burmese;
her poems appeared in Christian magazines.
JUNG: maiden name of Marianne von Willemer.

KAGO NO CHIYO: another name for Chiyoni.
KARSCH, ANNA LUISE (nee DURBACH): 1722-1791;
Nammer, Great Glogau, Berlin, Germany. a.k.a.
Die Deutsche Sappho, Die Karschin, and The
Prussian Sappho.
Work: poems published in 1764, 1772, 1792.
Orphaned, she became a farmer's wife and
worked as a milkmaid. She composed poetry
while she worked, wrote them down on Sundays.
Divorced after eleven years, she wandered as
an improvisatrice, began to sell her poems,
and opened a book shop. Several small pen-

sions were settled on her; two children and
a brother were all dependent on her.

KARSCHIN, DIE: nickname for Anna Luise Karsch.

KATAKO: see Daini no Sammi, under D.

KEMBLE: maiden name of Sarah Knight.

AL-KHANSA (AL-HANSA): fl. first half of 7th
century; Arabia.
Work: *I Tempi, La Vita e il Canzoniere Dell
Poetessa al-Hansa,* 1899; edited by G. Gab-
rielli; reprinted 1944.
She was the best known Arabic female poet,
famed for her elegies; elegy was regarded
among the ancient Arabs as a special pro-
vince of women.

KILLIGREW, ANN: 1660-1685; London, England.
Work: *Poems,* 1686; reprinted 1967, edited
by R. Morton.
She was well educated, showed early ability
in poetry and painting; served as maid of
honor to the Duchess of York; died of
smallpox, unmarried; her father published
her poems after her death.

KILLIGREW, CATHARINE (nee COOKE): 1530? - 1583;
Essex, England.
Work: Latin lines of verse on her grave.
Well educated with her three sisters, she
knew Hebrew, Greek and Latin; they were said
to be the equals of any man in that day; mar-
ried in 1565, she gave birth to a stillborn
child when she was in her fifties and died
six days later.

KINGSMILL: maiden name of Anne Finch.

KINNEY: maiden name of Julia H. Scott.

KLENK, VON: maiden name of Wilhelmina Christ-
iane von Chezy.

KNIGHT, ANN (nee CUTHBERT): 1790-1860; Montreal.
a.k.a. Fleming, her second married name.
Work: *A Year in Canada and Other Poems,*
1815; Edinburgh.
She was a prominent educator and writer in
Montreal for many years.

KNIGHT, ELLIS CORNELIA: 1757-1837; London,
Naples, Italy and the Continent.

Work: poetry, romances, journals and trans-
lations.
Educated at a school kept by a Swiss pastor,
she became proficient in Latin; she befrien-
ded the Hamiltons and Nelson while in Naples
and Rome, returned to England with them. She
became a Companion to Queen Charlotte and la-
ter the Princess Charlotte; Nelson called
her his Poet Laureate (to her embarrassment)
because of the verses she wrote of his vic-
tories.

KNIGHT, SARAH (nee KEMBLE): 1666-1727; Massachu-
setts, Connecticut. a.k.a. Madam Knight,
and Widow Knight.
Work: *The Journal of Madame Knight and Rev.
Mr. Buckingham,* 1825; contains her poetry.
She was well educated, a teacher, owned sev-
eral farms, kept a shop, speculated in In-
dian lands, was employed in the recording of
public documents (more than one hundred of-
ficial records bear her signature). Her
Journal is the result of a trip to New York
alone; married 1680, had one daughter; left
an estate valued at £1,800.

KOMACHI (ONO NO KOMACHI): 834-880; Japan.
Work: poems.
She was famed in her youth for beauty and
poetry; said to have died in poverty.

KOOLAART: maiden name or middle name of Elisa-
beth Hoofman.

KORINNA, KORINA: see Corinna.

KOWALSKA: maiden name of Elizabeth (Elzbieta)
Druzbacka.

KROMBALGH OF ALKMAAR: husband of Tesselschade
Visscher.

KUAN P'AN-P'AN: 8th or 9th century; Hsu Chou,
China.
Work: found in *The Orchid Boat,* pp. 15,
126-7.
She was a courtesan, became a concubine to
a statesman who built a "swallow" mansion
for her; they had a salon where they enter-
tained nobles; she committed suicide fif-

teen years after his death instead of imme-
diately, as society expected.
KUAN TAO-SHENG: 1262-1319; China.
Work: found in *The Orchid Boat*, pp. 53, 127.
She was famed as a calligrapher and painter
of bamboos, orchids and plum blossoms; mar-
ried to a leading calligrapher and painter
of Chinese history.

L: pseudonym of Letitia Landon.
LABANA: died c. 995; Cordova, Spain.
Work: poetry.
She was from a noble Arabic family, studied
philosophy and music.
LABE, LOUISE (nee CHARLIEU [CHARLY]): 1525-1566;
Lyon, France. a.k.a. Perrin, her married
name, and Captain Lays while in the army,
and La Belle Cordiere.
Work: *Oeuvres*, 1555; edited by C. Bou; and
The Love Sonnets, published in 1947, trans-
lated by F. Prohasch.
She knew Greek, Latin, Spanish and Italian;
she rode and practicised military exercises;
was fond of music, hunting and war; she ser-
ved in the army; married a wealthy ropemak-
er, thus her nickname The Beautiful Rope-
maker. She was the most important poet of
the sixteenth century in France; was out-
spoken in vindication of the rights of women
to develop their talents. She was given a
state funeral in Lyon.
LACTILLA: nickname for Anne Yearsley, who was a
milkwoman.
LADY, A: many of the poets in this Index pub-
lished their work under the pseudonym of
A Lady.
LAMB, MARY ANN: 1766-1847; London, England.
a.k.a. Sempronia, and Bridget Elia.
Work: *Poems for Children*, 1809, with her
brother Charles.
She supported her parents and brother by
dressmaking; spent thirteen years of her

life in mental institutions; she wrote four-
teen of the twenty *Tales from Shakespeare*
(Charles wrote six), but her name did not ap-
pear on the first six editions; her *Essay on
Needlework*, published in the British Ladies
Magazine in 1815, is an original piece which
places her among pioneers of economic
science; she had a modern grasp of women's
work in the home and society's dependence on
that work.
LANCASTER: see Philipa of Avis and Lancaster,
  under P.
LANDON, LETITIA ELIZABETH: 1802-1838; Chelsea,
  England and South Africa. a.k.a. MacLean,
  her married name, and L and L.E.L., pseu-
  donyms.
  Work: *Miscellaneous Poetical Works of L.E.
  L.*, 1835; *Life and Remains of L.E.L.*, 1841,
  two volumes; *Collected poems*, 1850, two vo-
  lumes, reprinted in 1873.
  Her poetry and novels were popular in her
  lifetime; well educated, she began to write
  early, and was published in newspapers; she
  died in South Africa shortly after her mar-
  riage, of an overdose of prussic acid.
LANNOY, JOHANNA CORNELIA DE (BARONESS): 1738-
  1782; Breda, Netherlands.
  Work: poems published in 1783, and plays.
  Self-taught, she won prizes for her poetry.
LAUNAY, LE VICOMTE DE: pen name of Delphine
  Girardin and her husband.
LAURA: pseudonym of Elizabeth Ferguson.
LAURA MARIA: pseudonym of Mary Robinson.
LAUREATE OF THE BLUESTOCKINGS: nickname for
  Hannah More.
L.E.L. pseudonym of Letitia Elizabeth Landon.
LEADBEATER, MARY (nee SCHACKLETON): 1758-1826;
  Kildare, Ireland.
  Work: *Poems*, 1808; *The Leadbeater Papers*.
  She was educated at home by a good tutor;
  married a pupil of her father's in 1791; was
  the village postmistress at Ballitore; had
  several children; narrowly escaped when the

French and Irish sacked Ballitore in 1798;
her poetry was published anonymously.

LEAPOR, MARY: 1722-1746; Northamptonshire, England.

Work: *Poems upon Several Occasions,* 1747; also
tragedy.
A domestic servant, her abilities exceeded
her rank and education; self-taught, her modesty kept her merit concealed until it was
too late for her to benefit; on her death
bed, she gave her father her manuscripts;
she died of measles.

LEE: maiden name of Anne Wharton.

LEE, MARY (LADY CHUDLEIGH); 1656-1710; Devonshire, England. a.k.a. Marissa in correspondence with Elizabeth Thomas, who was
called Corinna in their letters.
Work: *The Ladies' Defence,* 1701, a poem in
answer to a sermon; *Poems on Several Occasions,* 1703; posthumous editions of her
poems in 1713 and 1722.
Married in 1685, she was not happy; had
three children; she also wrote essays, tragedies, operas and masques.

LEE, SOPHIA: 1750-1824; London, England.
Work: poetry, novels, plays, ballads, and
tragedy. *The Hermit's Tale, Found in his
Cell,* 1787.
When her mother died, she took charge of
the household for her actor-father; from
the profits of an opera she wrote as a five
act play, she established a successful
school for young women!

LEGGE, ELIZABETH: 1580 - ?; England.
Work: poems.
Noted for acquiring languages, it was said
she became totally blind from severe study
and midnight reading.

LENNGREN, ANNA MARIA (nee MALMSTEDT): 1754-
1817; Upsala, Finland, and Stockholm, Sweden.
Work: *The Conseillen,* 1777, poked fun at
female follies; *Essays in Poesy,* 1819;

twelfth edition 1890; idylls, epigrams, and satirical verse published when she was eighteen.

The most important poet of her period, her poetry was published anonymously, often attributed to the leading male poets; she was honored by the Swedish Academy with a medal struck in her honor; she attacked upper classes with witty satire.

LENNOX, CHARLOTTE (nee RAMSEY): 1720-1804; New York and London.

Work: *Poems,* 1747; *Lady's Museum,* eleven editions; plays, and seven novels.

When she was a child, her father was Lt. Governor of New York; she was sent to England for her education; married, was left a widow with a child; she wrote for a living; she burlesqued the lengthy French Romances (especially Madelein de Scudery's) in *The Female Quixote,* 1752, she is sometimes called the first American novelist; received a pension from the Royal Literary Fund in her old age.

LEON: married name of Elizabeth Jane Weston.

LESCAILE, CATHARINE (KATHARINA LESCAILJE): 1649-1711; Amsterdam, Netherlands. a.k.a. The Tenth Muse.

Work: poems published in 1728; three volumes, 1731; also tragedies.

She continued her father's bookshop and printing office while writing poetry and translating plays.

LEVESQUE: maiden name of Maria-Louisa Rose Petigny.

LEVI, JUSTIN DE (nee PEROTTI): 14th century; Cremona, Italy. a.k.a. Puytendre, her married name.

Work: poems.

She was a contemporary and correspondent of of Petrarch; she wrote only in French so as not to rival the illustrious Petrarch.

LEWEN, VAN: maiden name of Letitia Pilkington.

LEWERS: maiden name of Mrs. Gray.

71

LI CH'ING-CHAO: 1084-1151; China.
Work: found in *The Orchid Boat*, pp. 36-44,
128.
Considered to be China's greatest female
poet, she came from a well known family of
scholars and officials; her mother was a
poet; she and her scholar husband spent most
of their money to collect seals, manuscripts,
calligraphy, and painting; they compiled the
best critical study and anthology of seals
and bronze characters; driven from their
home by Atars, they lost most of their col-
lection; the contents of ten buildings were
burned. Li is compared to Gaspara Stampa
and Louise Labe of the West.
LI YEH: 8th century; Ta'ang, China.
Work: found in *The Orchid Boat*, pp. 16 and
130.
She was a Taoist priestess, renowned for
beauty, wit, poetry, calligraphy and music;
when old, she was summoned to court.
LIGIER DE LA GARDE, DE: maiden name of Antoin-
ette Deshoulieres.
LINCOLN: first married name of Almira Phelps.
LINDSAY: maiden name of Anne Barnard.
LITTLE, SOPHIA: 1799 - ?; Rhode Island. a.k.a.
Rowena, her pseudonym.
Work: found in *The Female Poets of America*,
by Caroline May.
LITTLE SPITFIRE: nickname for Hester Chapone by
Richardson.
LIVERMORE, SARAH WHITE: 1789-1874; New Hampshire
Work: occasional verse.
LOCKE, JANE ERMINA: 1805-1859; Massachusetts.
Work: *Poems*, 1842; *Boston*, 1846, a poem;
The Recalled or Voices of the Past, 1855; and
Eulogy on the Death of Webster, 1855, rhymed.
LOGAN, DEBORAH (nee NORRIS): 1761-1839; Penn-
sylvania.
Work: poems found in *The Logan Letter Books*.
After girls' school, she continued educating
herself; married and had three sons. Her
transcript of the letters between Penn and

72

Logan, which she found in her attic, are a
source of importance to the history of early
Pennsylvania, published in 1870-72; she said
of the sonnet form, it is "putting the Muse
into corsets."

LOMBARDA: C. 1190; Provence, France.
Work: found in *The Women Troubadours*, pp.
114-17, 174-5.
Probably from Toulouse, the daughter of a
banker. (The name Lombard meant banker.)

LOUISE: pseudonym of Karoline Louise Brachman.

LOUVENCOURT, MARIE DE: 1680-1712; Paris.
Work: her songs were set to music by lead-
ing composers of her day.

LUCAS: maiden name of Margaret Cavendish.

LUCCHESINI, GUIDICCIONI LAURA: fl. 1601; Sienna,
Italy.
Work: lyrics; three pastorals set to music.

LUCINDA CORITESEA: name of AURORA GAETANS in
the Arcadia Academia.

LUTEL: maiden name of Madame Dumont.

LYNCH: middle name of Hester Thrale.

MA HSIANG-LAN: 16th century; Chin Ling (Nan-
king), China. a.k.a. Ma Shou-Chen.
Work: found in *The Orchid Boat*, pp. 63, 130.
She was a leading courtesan, a painter of
orchids.

MA SHOU-CHEN: another name for Ma Hsiang-Lan.

MaCARTNEY: maiden name of Frances Greville.

MacLEAN: married name of Letitia E. Landon.

MacVICAR: maiden name of Anne Grant.

MAD MADGE: popular name for Margaret Cavendish.

MADAM KNIGHT: popular name for Sarah Kemble
Knight.

MADISON, DOROTHEA (nee PAYNE): 1768-1849; Vir-
ginia and North Carolina. a.k.a. Todd, her
first married name; Dolley, her nickname; and
Dowager or Queen Dowager, Nation's Hostess,
Quaker Dolley, and Queen Dolley.
Work: *The Dolley Madison Collection*, thir-
teen volumes, Library of Congress; also,

occasional poems, letters amd memoirs.
The First Lady during the Presedencies of
James, her husband, and Jefferson, a widow-
er, she saved state documents when the White
House was burned in 1812. She was raised a
Quaker; her father freed his slaves. Though
famous as a hostess, she never learned to
dance.

MADRE, LA and LA MADRE CASTILLO: nicknames for
Francisca Josefa del Castillo y Guevara, un-
der C.

MAGDEBURG, VON: see Mechthild.

MAINE, DUCHESSE DU: title of Anne Louise Bene-
dicte de Bourbon.

MALEPIERRA, OLYMPIA: died 1559; Venice, Italy.
Works; poems published at Naples.

MALESCOTTE, MARGHERITA: died 1720; Sienna,
Italy.
Work: poems.

MALMSTEDT: maiden name of Anna Maria Lenngren.

MANLEY: maiden name of Emma Catherine Embury.

MANNERS, ELIZABETH (nee SIDNEY) COUNTESS RUT-
LAND: died 1615; England.
Work: poems.
Married in 1599, she bore no children; she
was said to be "nothing inferior" to her
father, Sir Philip Sidney.

MANZONI, GIUSTI FRANCESCA: died 1743; Milan,
Italy.
Work: *An Epistle in Verse to the Empress
Maria Theresa;* tragedies, sacred dramas, or-
atorio, translations.
She was a member of the academy Filodossi at
Milan.

MAPPELLI: married name of Cassandra Fedele.

MARATTI: maiden name of Faustina Zappi.

MARGARET OF FRANCE (QUEEN OF NAVARRE & VALOIS):
1552-1615; France.
Work: poems, memoirs.
She lived a stormy life amidst the struggles
for Protestantism in France; said to have
written and spoken better than any woman of
her time. She gave a tenth of her money to

the poor but did not pay her bills.
MARGARET OF NAVARRE (VALOIS, D'ANGOULEME, ALEN-
   CON): 1492-1549; France.
   a.k.a. The Tenth Muse, The Pearl; Parlamente
   in her own book *Heptameron*.
   Work: *Les Marguerites del lan Marguerite
   des Princesses,* (The Pearls of the Pearl of
   Princesses), poetry, 1547; *Heptameron, or
   Novels of Queen of Navarre,* 1558; also let-
   ters, comedies, moralities.
   First married to Duke of Alencon, then Henry
   d'Albret; held court at Pau and Nerac where
   she was patron to literature and the Refor-
   mation; she wrote in defense of women, pro-
   posed chastity without prudery that would
   reconcile marriage with love for the honor
   and happiness of women; she is one of the
   earliest representatives of personal poetry
   who laid bare her inmost meditations.
MARGARET OF SAVOI (SAVOY): 1523-1574; France.
   Work: poems.
   She was a niece of Margaret of Navarre, 1492-
   1549, and a patron of poets.
MARGARET OF SCOTLAND: c. 1425-1445; Scotland.
   Work: rondeaux.
   She considered herself a pupil of Alain
   Chartier.
MARI NIGHEAN ALISDAIR RUAIDH (MARY, THE DAUGHTER
   OF RED ALEXANDER): 16th century, Ireland.
   Work: poems and songs.
   She was a bard, a member of professional pub-
   lic singers; they were bound by oath to sing
   only true accounts, and were highly respect-
   ed by their clans. When James came to the
   throne, an edict was issued against them, but
   Mari, because of her popularity, was allowed
   to stay and given a pension; she in turn
   sheltered wandering bards until she also was
   banished. Forbidden to sing songs, she in-
   vented *croons* and sang her way back home.
MARIA ABI JOCOBI ALFARSULI: 11th century; Se-
   ville, Spain. a.k.a. de Marien.
   Work: various epigrams.

Her father was Jocobi Alfarsuli; she may be
the same poet as Maria Alphaizuli (the dif-
ference in dates may be due to the differ-
ences between Mohamedan and Gregorian Calen-
ders).

MARIA, BERNARDA: 17th century; Seville, Spain.
Work: poetry.

MARIA DE HISPALI: c. 1039; Seville, Spain.
Work: poetry.
She may be the same poet as Maria Alfarsuli,
above.

MARIA DE VENTADORN (nee DE TURENNE): c. 1165;
Provence, France.
Work: found in *The Woman Troubadours*, pp.
98-9 and 168-9.
She was a patron of troubadours and a pre-
cursor to the dame de salon.

MARIA DEL OCCIDENTE: nickname for Maria Gowen
Brooks.

MARIA JUANA: fl. 18th century; Lima, Peru.
Work: poetry.

MARIE DE FRANCE (MARY): fl. 1165; France and
England.
Work: *Lais*, short narrative poems based on
folk love themes; *Ysopet (Esopet, Isopet,
Usopet)* fables.
The earliest known female poet of France,
she wrote in Anglo-Norman dialect, but lived
in England. She was well educated, her en-
lightened opinions show courage in speaking
the truth; her identity is uncertain.

MARIEN, DE: name for Maria Abi Jocobi Alfarsuli.

MARIN DE SOLAR, MERCEDES: 1804-1866; Chile. a.
k.a. La Musa de la Caridad Christiana (The
Muse of Christian Charity), by Bello.
Work: *Poesias de la Senora Dona Mercedes
Marin Del Solar, descuellen: Canto Fumelre,
Canto a la Caridad Dulce es morir, y Pleg-
aria al Pie de la Cruz.*
She wrote an elegy in outrage at the murder
of Diego Portales in 1836, which became pop-
ular in Peru, Colombia, Brazil and Argentina,
as well as her native Santiago.

MARINELLI, LUCREZIA: 1571-1653; Venice, Italy.
Work: *La Nobilita e la Eccellenza Della Donne, con Defetti E Manecamenti Degli Uomini,* (The Excellence of Women and the Defects of Men), 1601, Venice. Also poetry, history, lives of saints, letters, and sculpture.

MARISSA: pseudonym of Mary Lee, Lady Chudleigh.

MARQUETS, ANNE DE: died 1558; France.
Work: three hundred and eighty religious sonnets.
A nun, she bequeathed her sonnets to Sister Marie de Fortia; she became blind before death.

MARSHALL: maiden name of Isabella Graham.

MARTIN, SARAH: 1791-1843; Caister, England.
Work: *Selections from the Poetical Remains of Sarah Martin,* 1845; also short lyrics grouped as *The Sick Room.*
A dressmaker by trade, she began visiting prisons to improve the condition of the prisoners; she taught them to read and write with the scriptures; wrote text books for this work; it was twelve years before any other group or individual took an interest in her work; do to her efforts, deplorable prison conditions were eventually improved.

MARTINEAU, HARRIET: 1802-1876; Norwich, England.
Work: a prolific writer, she wrote poetry, short stories, novels, travelogues, history, culture,philosophy, anti-slavery, autobiography; twenty-five volumes on economics; ten volumes on law; five on taxation!
In spite of being deaf and having no sense of taste or smell, this remarkable woman led an active life as a journalist; by 1829, she was supporting her mother and sister by needlework; her first books on economics were turned down by publishers but were printed through subscription and were very popular; her economic books were censured in Russia; her comments on American slavery un-

popular in the U.S.; she wrote sixty arti-
cles against licensed brothels in India. Told
she was hopelessly ill in 1854, she wrote her
autobiography! She lived for twenty-two more
years, refusing a government pension.

MARY, THE DAUGHTER OF RED ALEXANDER: see Mari
Nighean Alisdair Ruaidh.

MARY: fl. 4 B.C.; Nazareth, Israel. a.k.a. The
Mother of Jesus, Virgin Mary, Mother of God,
Protector of Pilgrims, et cetera.
Work: *My Soul Magnifies the Lord*, Luke 1:46
to 1:55, The Bible. This work is also call-
ed *The Magnificat*, and *Hymn of the Blessed
Virgin*.

MARY OF FRANCE: English version of Marie de
France.

MARY OF THE GAEL: popular name for Saint Bridget
of Kildare.

MARY, QUEEN OF SCOTS (STUART): 1542-1587; Scot-
land, France and England.
Work: poems in French and Latin.
Sent to France at the age of six to be rais-
ed with the French royal children, she mar-
ried Francois II in 1558 who died soon after
coming to the throne; she married Lord Darn-
ley in 1565, Bothwell in 1567; she became
Queen of Scotland when only six days old; as
a contender for the English crown, she became
an unfortunate pawn in international and re-
ligious wars; she was executed by Queen Eli-
zabeth I after eighteen years imprisonment
in England.

MARY GODOLPHIN: pseudonym of Lucy Aikin.

MARY SINGLETON: pseudonym of Frances Brooke.

MASQUIERES, FRANCOISE: died 1728; France.
Work: poems.

MATCHLESS ORINDA: nickname for Katherine Phil-
ips.

MATRAINI, CLARA (CHIARA) CANTARINI: fl. 1562;
Lucca, Italy.
Work: *Poems*, 1560, Venice; also poetry in
her letters, 1595.
Skilled in Platonic philosophy, sacred his-

tory and poetry, she was one of the best poets of her time.

MATTUGANI: another spelling for Bartolomea Mattugliani.

MATTUGLIANI, BARTOLOMEA: 15th century, Bologna, Italy. a.k.a. Mea.
Work: one poem extant.
Her one poem is a reply to Carlo Cavalcabo in terza rima, in which she gives an account of those women who have honored their sex by their virtue.

McCARTNEY: middle name of Louisa Crawford.

MEA: popular name for Bartolomea Mattugliani.

MECHTHILD VON MAGDEBURG: c. 1212- c. 1280; Germany.
Work: *Das Fliessende Licht der Gottheit,* the original in low German was lost, but it is preserved in a 1344 High German version; reprinted in 1869 and 1929; prayers mixed with prose and verse.

MEDAGLIA: maiden name of Diamante Faini.

MEEKE, MARY (nee GABRIELLI?): died 1816; Staffordshire, England. a.k.a. Gabrielli, possible pseudonym.
Work: *Poems,* 1782; six novels, translations from French and German; *Correspondence of Madame du Deffand,* 1810; two volumes. She edited these previously unpublished works.

MEGALOSTRATA: 668 B.C.; Sparta, Greece.
Work: no poetry extant but satires were written against her that show that her talents were known and envied.

MELICA: surname of Theano Locrencis, under T.

MELISSA: pen name of Jane Brereton.

MELVILLE, ELIZABETH (LADY CULROSS): fl. 1603; Scotland. a.k.a. Colvill, her married name.
Work: *Ane Godlie Dreame Compylit in Scottish Meter be M.M., Gentilwoman in Culross, at the Request of her Freindes,* Edinburgh, 1603.
Identity of author uncertain: M.M. may stand for Mistress Melvill; the book went through several editions in the seventeenth and

eighteenth centuries.

MENDOZA: see Luisa de Carvajal y Mendoza, under C.

MENDOZA, ANTONIA DE (CONDESA DE BENEVENTE): died 1656; Seville, Spain.
Work: poems, motets, madrigals, romances, glosas, sonnets, elegies and comedies.
She was a lady to Isabel of Borbon, and Mariana de Austria.

MENDOZA, ELVIRA DE: 16th century, Santo Domingo.
Work: poetry.

MENG CHU: 3rd century, China.
Work: found in *The Orchid Boat*, pp. 8, 130. Ten verses are attributed to her, but they are probably ancient folk songs from what are today the provinces of Hunan and Hupei.

MERCER, MARGARET: 1791-1846; Maryland. a.k.a. Hannah More of America.
Work: poetry and essays.
She was also an educator and abolitionist, an active proponent of female education. On the death of her father, she freed the family slaves, then sold the property to buy and free other slaves for resettlement in Liberia! Forced to support herself, she founded a school for girls; she also promoted Sunday Schools.

MERKEN, VAN: maiden name of Lucretia Wilhelmina Winter.

MEXICAN NUN: popular name for Juana Ines de la Cruz.

MEYSEY-WIGLEY: maiden name of Caroline Clive.

MIDA, MIDE, MEDEA: other spellings for the Irish Saint Ita.

MILLER: maiden name of Margaret Davidson.

MILLER, ANNA (nee RIGGS) (LADY): 1741-1781; Bath-Easton, England.
Work: *Letters from Italy*, 1770-71, and 1777; *On Novelty, and on Trifles and Triflers*, 1778; also poems.
She brought a large fortune to her marriage in 1765; he adopted her maiden surname before his own; they lived in France and Italy;

later at Bath-Easton where she had a salon;
they held poetry contests and crowned win-
ners with laurel; Anna Seward developed in
this salon, but Lady Miller was much sati-
rized by other writers.

MIRA BAI: c. 1420; India.
Work: poems in honor of Krishna in the Braj
Bhasha, the Hindi dialect of West Hindustan.
She was a Rajput Princess.

MIREMONT: married name of Gabrielle de Coignard.

MITFORD, MARY RUSSELL: 1787-1855; Hampshire,
England. a.k.a. Sancho Panza in Petticoats,
by Letitia E. Landon.
Work: *Poems*, 1806; *Miscellaneous Poems*,
1810; *Christina the Ward of the South Seas*,
narrative poem; *Blanche, a Spanish Story*,
narrative poem; *Narrative Poems on Female
Character*, 1813; *Dramatic Scenes*, sonnets,
1827. Also sketches, tragedies, stories, and
an autobiography.
Her father dissipated several fortunes, in-
cluding one of her own; she was forced to
support her family; she is sometimes cred-
ited with having invented the sketch as a
literary form; her correspondence with Amer-
ican authors made her a tie between Old and
New England.

MODERATA FONTE: pseudonym of Modesta Pazzo.

MOENS, PETONELLA: 1762-1843; Netherlands.
Work: *De Ware Christen*, 1785; *J. de Groot*,
1790. *Winterlavern*, 1820. Also prose, most-
ly children's books.
She was blind from the age of four.

MOERO (MYRO): c. 300 B.C.; Byzantium.
Work: epic, lyric and elegiac poems.
She is one of the nine poets named by Anti-
pater of Thessalonica in the *Greek Anthology;*
she was the mother of tragic poet Homerus.

MOINA: pseudonym of Anna Dinnies.

MOISE, PENINA: 1797-1880; United States.
Work: poetry.

MOLESWORTH: maiden name of Mary Monk (Monck).

MOLSA (MOLZA), TARQUINIA: fl. 1600; Rome, Italy.

Work: poems.
She was educated with her brothers by the
best teachers of literature and science; the
city of Rome by a decree of the Senate in
which all her excellencies were set forth,
honored her with the title of Singular, and
bestowed on her and the family of Molsa the
rights of Roman citizenship, an unusual hon-
or to be conferred on a woman: passed 1600.
MONCURE: maiden name of Jean Wood.
MONK (MONCK), MARY (nee MOLESWORTH): died 1715;
Ireland.
Work: *Marinda: Poems and Translations on
Several Occasions,* 1716; London.
Self-educated, she knew Spanish, Italian, and
Latin; her only help in writing was a large
library; she had a large family; her poems
were published after her death.
MONTAGUE, THE AMERICAN: popular name for Sarah
Morton.
MONTAGUE, MARY WORTLEY (nee PIERREPONT): 1689-
1762; England and Italy. Pope called her
The Furious Sappho.
Work: *The Poetical Works of Lady Mary Wort-
ley Montague,* 1768; also five volumes of let-
ters.
Irregularly educated and brought up in seclu-
sion, she was able to develop her mind in a
way rare for women of the period; she mar-
ried in 1712; they lived in Turkey for a
year, where she had her children innoculated
against smallpox; she later introduced the
practice in England. She believed education
was the key to female emancipation.
MONTEGUT, JEANNE DE SEGLA, MADAME DE: 1709 - ?;
Toulouse, France.
Work: books published at Paris in 1768 in-
clude poetry, translations, and letters.
She won the prize for poetry three times at
the Floral Games of Toulouse.
MONTENAY, GEORGETTE: fl. 1574; Navarre, France.
Work: one hundred emblems on Christian or
moral subjects, illustrated with her own

verses, dedicated to Jeanne d'Albret.
She lost her entire family to the plague;
Jeanne d'Albret (daughter of Margaret of Na-
varre) took her in as maid of honor.

MONTGEROULT DE COUTANCES, ANNE MARIE (COMTESSE D'
HAUTPOUL): 1760-1837; France.
Work: poetry, novels, pastoral romances,
tales.
Her romances were partly in verse, partly
prose.

MONTGOMERY, COUNTESS: title of Mary Sidney
Wroth.

MOODIE, SUSANNA (nee STRICKLAND): 1803-1885;
England and Canada.
Work: *Enthusiasm and Other Poems*, 1830;
Roughing it in the Bush, 1852, contains
verse; two volumes.
She was one of the four famous Strickland
sisters, all writers; she married in 1831,
emigrated to Canada in 1832; they founded a
literary monthly; she wrote novels to sup-
port the family, had seven children.

MOODY: maiden name of Catherine Grace Frances
Gore.

MOORE: maiden name of Frances Brooke.

MORE, HANNAH: 1745-1833; Gloucestershire and
London, England. a.k.a. The Laureate of the
Bluestockings, and Stella, the name given her
by Anne Yearsley.
Work: *Bas Bleu*, 1786, about the Bluestock-
ings; *Works*, 1801, eleven volumes, re-
printed in 1830.
One of the original Bluestockings, she was
given the rudiments of a classical education
by her father, who at the same time feared
educated women, so counteracted his own les-
sons; she and her sisters spent their entire
lives working for female education; her
first play, published when she was sixteen,
began sixty-three years of literary life; she
earned L30,000, left L10,000 to charity; she
was abused by landowners and clergy for help-
ing the poor.

MORELLI: maiden name of Maria Maddalena Fernan-
dez.

MORGAN, SYDNEY OWENSON: 1783-1859; Ireland and
London. a.k.a. Glorvina.
Work: *Woman and her Master: a Philosophi-
cal History to the Fall of the Roman Empire*,
1840; also, poetry, Irish songs, novels,
comic operas, travel books, biographies and
autobiography.
Published poetry as a child, her first novel
at sixteen; she was called Glorvina after the
heroine of her most popular book, *The Wild
Irish Girl*; married reluctantly in 1812; tra-
velled extensively in France and Italy; re-
ceived the first pension given to a woman
"in acknowledgement of the services rendered
by her to the world of letters."

MORPURGO, RAHEL: 1790-1871; Trieste.
Work: *Ugab Rahel*, edited by I. Castiglione;
poems and letters, 1890.
She wrote mostly songs for special occasions,
translated from French and Italian; was cal-
led the first modern Hebrew poetess.

MORTON, SARAH WENTWORTH (nee APTHORPE): 1759-
1846; Boston, Massachusetts. a.k.a. Constan-
tia, Philenia, and A Lady of Boston (pseudo-
nyms); and The American Sappho, and The Amer-
ican Montague (nicknames).
Work: *Ouabi, or the Virtues of Nature*, a
poem, 1790; *Beacon Hill, Local Poems, His-
toric and Descriptive*, 1797; and *My Mind &
Its Thoughts*, 1823; prose and poetry.
She was the foremost woman of her generation,
one of the Della Cruscan poets; her poems
were read in England as well as America; she
designed her own home, outlived all her five
children and near relatives.

MOTHER OF GOD: popular name for Mary, the Mother
of Jesus.

MOTTE: see Jeanne Marie Bouvier de la Motte Gu-
yon, under G.

MULSO: maiden name of Hester Chapone.

MUNTER: maiden name of Frederika Brun.

MURASAKI, SHIKIBU: c. 978-1031; Japan. Real
    name unknown.
    Work: *Genji Monogatari* (Tale of Genji): six
    volumes; 1925-1933, in English; a new one
    volume edition printed 1952; *Murasaki Shi-
    kibu Kashu*, her collected poems; and *Muri-
    saki Shikibu Nikki*, her diary.
    She was a member of the powerful Fujiwara
    clan; served the Empress Akiko; was well
    known as a poet; *Genji* is the oldest full-
    length novel in the world; she was one of
    many great women writers in that period,
    when men rarely ventured into literature.
MURAT, DE: married name of Henrietta Julie de
    Castelnau.
MURPHY: maiden name of Anna Brownell Jameson.
MURRY, ANN: fl. 1778-1799; England.
    Work: *Mentoria: or the Young Ladies Instruc-
    tor*, 1778; *The Sequel to Mentoria*, 1799; and
    Poems on Various Subjects, 1779, by subscrip-
    tion.
MUSA DE LA CARIDAD CRISTIANA, LA: name for Mer-
    cedes Marin de Solar.
MUSE: from Greek mythology, the Muses were nine
    young women who inspired poetry, music,
    dance, history, and astronomy.
MUSE DE LA PATRIE: nickname for Delphine Gi-
    rardin.
MUSE OF CUMBERLAND: popular name for Susanna
    Blamire.
MUSE LIMONADIERE, LA: nickname for Charlotte
    Bourette.
MYRO: another spelling for Moero.
MYRTIS: fl. 500 B.C.; Boeotia, Greece.
    Work: none extant. Plutarch gives an ex-
    tract of her poem on the Boeotian hero Eunos-
    tus.
    She taught Corinna and Pindar; was called
    the Sweet Singing Myrtis in the *Greek Antho-
    logy*, where she is one of nine female poets
    named by Antipater of Thessalonica.

85

NAIRNE, CAROLINA (nee OLIPHANT) (OLIFARD) LADY:
1766-1845; Perthshire, Scotland and Ireland.
a.k.a. B.B., Mrs. Bogan of Bogan, S.M., The
Scottish Minstrel, and Flower of Strathearn.
Work: *The Scottish Minstrel*, 1824, six oc-
tavo volumes, various editions have eighty-
seven of her songs plus Scottish songs. *Lays
from Strathearn*, 1846, published under her
real name.
She refused to sign her real name to poetry;
even her husband did not know she was writ-
ing; her publisher did not know her name or
where she lived; her poetry was often attri-
buted to Burns; she is said to have written
the finest lyrics in the Scottish language,
and over seventy of the best songs ever com-
posed.
NAKATSUKASA, LADY: c. 970; Japan.
Work: found in anthologies of tanka.
NAKIKA: the real name of Sei Shonagon.
NATION'S HOSTESS: nickname for Dorothea Madison.
NAVARRE, QUEEN OF: see Margaret of Navarre, 1492-
1549; and Margaret of France, 1552-1615.
NEGRO SAPPHO: popular name for Phillis Wheatley.
NEUVILLE, DE: married name of Magdalen de L'Au-
bespine.
NEVARES, MARTA DE: mentioned as possible iden-
tity for Amarilis.
NEVEU: maiden name of Madeleine Desroches.
NEWCASTLE, DUCHESS: title of Margaret Cavendish.
NICOSTRATA: possibley another name for Carmenta.
NIEH SHENG-CH'IUNG: Sung Dynasty, Ch'ang An,
China.
Work: found in *The Orchid Boat*, pp.49 and
130.
She was a courtesan.
NIJO, LADY: 1258-1306?; Kyoto, Japan.
Work: *Towazugatari (Confessions of Lady Ni-
jo)*, rediscovered in 1940 by a Japanese scho-
lar; translated into English by Karen Bra-
zell, 1973.
Raised in the Imperial Court, concubine to
the Emperor at fourteen, her *Confessions*

86

(autobiography with poetry) reveal humor and
humanity quite contrary to our expectations
of Oriental harem life; Nijo had lovers and
love affairs enough; expelled from court at
twenty-six, she became a Buddhist nun; tra-
velled the rest of her life.

NOGAROLA ARCO D'ANGELA: 15th century; Verona,
Italy.
Work: a metrical translation of books from
the Bible; letters.

NORDEN-FLEICHT (NORDENFLYCHT) CHEDERIG CHARLOTTE
(HEDVIG CHARLOTTA): 1718-1793; Stockholm,
Sweden.
Work: *The Mourning Turtle Dove*, 1743; *An
Apology for Women*, poem; *Samlade Skrifter*,
three volumes; 1924-38.
She began writing poetry after the death of
her husband; her home became a literary meet-
ing place, the first in Sweden; she was one
of three principal representatives of the
wave of pessimism which followed the ration-
alistic optimism of Dalein.

NORNA: pseudonym of Mary Elizabeth Brooks.

NORRIS: maiden name of Deborah Logan.

NOSSIS: 290 B.C.: Locri, Italy.
Work: twelve Doric epigrams in the *Greek
Anthology*.
All her epigrams relate to the cult of Aphro-
dite in which she was a priestess; she com-
pares herself to Sappho; she was called the
"tender voiced," in an epigram by Antipater.

OAKES: middle name of Elizabeth Oakes Smith.

OAKES SMITH: pseudonym of Elizabeth Oakes Smith.

OCHS, VON: maiden name of Philippine Amalie
Elise von Hohenhauser.

OE SHIKIBU: real name of Izumi Shikibu.

OGILVY: middle name of Elizabeth Benger.

OGLE: maiden name of Barbarina Brand.

OLIPHANT: maiden name of Carolina Nairne.

OLYMPIA, CORILLA: name of Maria Maddalena Fer-
nandez in the Arcadia.

O NEIL, HENRIETTA (nee DUNGARVON): 1758-1793;
    Ireland.
    Work: poems found in *Elegiac Sonnets and
    Other Essays,* edited by Charlotte Smith, five
    editions, 1784, 1789.
ONO NO KOMACHI: listed under K.
OPIE, AMELIA (nee ALDERSON): 1769-1853; Norwich,
    England.
    Work: *The Father and the Daughter,* 1801 and
    later editions; *The Warrior's Return and Oth-
    er Poems,* 1808; *Lays for the Dead,* 1834.
    Her novel *Adelina Mobray,* 1804, is a satiri-
    cal story based on the life of Mary Woll-
    stonecraft; she joined the Society of Friends
    in 1825; partially withdrew from society af-
    ter that; her songs were popular.
ORINDA: pseudonym of Katherine Philips.
ORLANDINE, EMILIA: fl. 1726; Sienna, Italy.
    Work: her poems are to be found in various
    collections.
OTIS: maiden name of Mercy Warren.
OVANDO, LEONOR DE (SOR): died after 1609; Santo
    Domingo.
    Work: six poems preserved by Dona Elvira de
    Mendoza.
    She is the first poet of the New World, a
    member of the Convent of the church Regina
    de la Espanola, in Santo Domingo.
OWENSON: maiden name of Sydney Morgan.

PACKARD, CLARISSA: pen name of Caroline Howard
    Gilman.
PAGAN, ISOBEL: 1740-1821; Ayrshire, Scotland.
    a.k.a. Tibby, a nickname.
    Work: *Collection of Songs and Poems,* 1805;
    GLasgow.
    Lame from infancy, she was nevertheless the
    hostess of an inn where she had an unlicens-
    ed traffic in liquor and evening parties
    where verses were recited; she wrote uncouth
    lyrics, tributes to friends and references to
    sport on autumn moors.

PALEOTI, IPPOLITA: 16th century; Bologna, Italy.
Work: poems in Greek and Latin.
PALMER: middle name of Elizabeth Peabody.
PAN CHAO: c. 45 - c. 115; China.
Work:*Lessons for Women,* 106; also, poetry.
She was commissioned by the Emperor to com-
plete the history of the former Han Dynasty;
she wrote a treatise on astronomy; she was a
respected teacher at court.
PAN CHIEH-YU: 1st century B.C.: China.
Work: found in *The Orchid Boat,* pp. 3, 131.
Her name was a title of honor given to the
Imperial concubine, her real name is unknown;
later she was removed when she fell out of
favor, became an attendant to the Emperor's
mother, and later at the Imperial tombs.
PANNOLINI, FEBRONIA: 16th century; Bologna,
Italy.
Work: hymns and prose in Latin and Italian.
PAO LING-HUI: 5th century, China.
Work: found in *The Orchid Boat,* pp.13, 131.
She was the younger sister of Pao Chao (414-
466).
PAOLINI, MASSINI PETRONELLA: 1663-1726; Aquila
and Rome, Italy. a.k.a. Fidelma Partenide
in the Arcadia Academia.
Work: canzonetts, sonnets, poems and drama.
PARK: maiden name of Louisa Jane Hall.
PARKER: middle name of Eliza Townsend.
PARKHOUSE: maiden name of Hannah Cowley.
PARLAMENTE: Margaret of Navarre in her own book,
Heptameron.
PARTENIDE, FEDELMA: name of Petronella Paolini
in the Arcadia.
PARTENIDE, IRMINDA: name of Luisa Bergalli in
the Arcadia Academia.
PARTHENAI (PARTHENAY), CATHARINE DE: 1554-1631;
France. a.k.a. her first married name, Quel-
lence; renamed Soubise; her second married
name Renatus.
Work: poetry published in 1572; also trage-
dies, comedies, satire.
She was devoted to Calvinism; lost her first

husband at the massacre of Saint Bartholo-
mew's Day; after the death of her second hus-
band, she devoted her life to the education
of her children; at age seventy-five, she
was imprisoned in the Castle of Niort, died
two years later.

PASTON, MARGERY (MARGARET) (nee BREWS): died c.
1495; Norwich and Norfolk, England.
Work: poems found in letters to her future
husband, John Paston, the younger (died 1503)
preserved in the Paston Family Correspon-
dence, 1422-1507.

PATACIC, KATARINA: 18th century; Croatia.
Work: *Pesme Karvatske*, 1781; poems in Kaj-
kavski dialect.
Her poetry shows Italian influence and baro-
que style.

PATRIE, LA MUSE DE LA: nickname of Delphine Gi-
rardin.

PAYNE: maiden name of Dorothea (Dolley) Madison.

PAZZO, MODESTA: 1555-1592; Venice, Italy. a.k.a.
Moderata Fonte, her pseudonym.
Work: poems, *Il Floridoro*, and *Passion and
Resurrection of Jesus Christ;* also prose.
Orphaned in infancy, placed in a convent but
later moved out and married; she knew Latin,
and memorized sermons; her prose, *Dei Meriti
Delle Donne*, maintains that women are not
inferior to men intellectually.

PEABODY, ELIZABETH PALMER: 1804-1894; Massachu-
setts. a.k.a. Grandmother of Boston, and the
Grandmother of the Kindergarten.
Work: poetry.
She was also a publisher, shop keeper, edu-
cator and social reformer. She mastered ten
languages, learned Polish at sixty; conduct-
ed two private schools before she was twenty;
founded a school for deaf mutes and the
first kindergarten in the U.S. in 1860, She
was an abolitionist and suffragist; her shop
with foreign books in Boston became a lit-
erary center.

PEARL, THE: nickname of Margaret of Navarre,

1492-1549.

PECH, DE: see de Pech de Calage, under C.

PEMBROKE, COUNTESS; title of Mary Herbert.

PENDARVES: first married name of Mary Delany.

PERDITA: name of Mary Robinson in correspondence
with the Prince of Wales, later George IV.

PERFECT MAID: sometime translation of Accom-
plished maid of Tuscany.

PEROTTI: maiden name of Justin de Levy.

PERRIN: married name of Louise Labe.

PESCARA, MARQUISE DE: married name of Vittoria
Colonna.

PET MARJORIE: nickname for Marjorie (Margaret)
Fleming.

PETERS: married name of Phillis Wheatley.

PETIGNY, MARIA-LOUISE ROSE (nee LEVESQUE): 1768-
?; Paris, France. a.k.a. Petite Fille, by
Gessner.
Work: *Idylles*, other occasional verse.

PEYRE: middle name of Anna Dinnies.

PHALIER: see Francoise Therese Aumile de Sainte-
Phalier, under S.

PHANTASIA: 12th B.C.; Memphis, Egypt.
Work: poems on the Trojan War and Ulysses'
return.
Chiron says she wrote a poem on the Trojan
War, and another on the return of Ulysses to
Ithaca from which Homer copied the greater
part of the Iliad and Odyssey when he visit-
ed Memphis where the poems were deposited.

PHELPS, ALMIRA (nee HART): 1793-1884; Connecti-
cut, New York, Vermont, Pennsylvania and
Maryland. a.k.a. Lincoln, her first married
name.
Work: poetry; also textbooks on chemistry,
botany, education, geology and natural philo-
sophy.
Widowed at thirty, with two children, she be-
gan to study; taught at her sister's (Emma
Willard) Troy Female Seminary; remarried in
1831; spent the next six years in Vermont
writing her text books; became head of sev-
eral women's schools; her *Familiar Lectures*

on Botany went through nine editions in ten
years, sold 275,000 copies in 1872; she was
the second female member of the American As-
sociation for the Advancement of Science.
PHILENIA: another pseudonym of Sarah Wentworth
Morton.
PHILIPA OF AVIS AND LANCASTER, PRINCESS: 1437-
1497; Portugal.
Work: poems.
She entered the convent of Odivellas near
Lisbon.
PHILIPS, JOAN: fl. 1679; England. Possible i-
dentity of Ephelia.
Work: *Female Poems on Several Occasions*, by
Ephelia, 1679.
She is mentioned as possibly being the daugh-
ter of Katherine Philips.
PHILIPS, KATHERINE (nee FOWLER): 1631-1664; Lon-
don, Wales and Dublin. a.k.a. Orinda, pseu-
donym; The Matchless Orinda, and The English
Sappho, nicknames.
Work: an unauthorized edition of her poems,
1664; authorized version, *Poems by the Most
Deservedly Admired Mrs. Katherine Philips,
the Matchless Orinda*, 1667; letters.
Poems prefaced to the works of others esta-
blished her literary reputation; her plays
in translation from French were successful.
Her son died when he was only fourty days
old; her daughter, Katherine, was born in
1656. She had a salon, was an ardent propo-
nent of friendship between women. She died
of smallpox in an epidemic.
PHILOMEL: name for Susanna Wright by James Lo-
gan.
PHILOMELA: pseudonym of both Elizabeth Rowe and
Mercy Warren.
PHILOTHEA: name for Lydia Maria Child by Lowell.
PHOENIX OF MEXICO (FENIX DE MEXICO): see Juana
Ines de la Cruz.
PIERIAN BEE: popular name for Sappho.
PIERRE, BOIS DE LA: under B for Bois.
PIERREPONT: maiden name of Mary Wortley Monta-

gue.

PILKINGTON, LETITIA (nee VAN LEWEN): 1712-1751;
    Ireland and England.
    Work: *Memoirs of Mrs. Laetitia Pilkington,
    Written by Herself, Wherein are Occasionally
    Interspersed All Her Poems, With Anecdotes
    of Several Eminent Persons Living and Dead,*
    1748; third edition, 1754; *The Celebrated Mrs.
    Pilkington's Jests, or, the Cabinet of Wit &
    Humour,* 1751; poems, memoirs, comedy and tra-
    gedy.
    Separated from her husband, she was support-
    ed by contributions for awhile, but then
    thrown into debtors prison; she later opened
    a shop for printing pamphlets which was suc-
    cessful.

PILKINGTON, MARY (nee HOPKINS): 1766-1839; Eng-
    land.
    Work: *Original Poems,* 1811; also prose, nov-
    els, and tales.
    She worked as a governess in a private fam-
    ily; after the publication of her first book,
    she became a prolific writer, which support-
    ed her after a disabling illness in 1810.

PIMENTEL, MADAME: fl. 1790; Naples, Italy.
    Work: poetry.
    She is described as a poet living in Naples
    at the time of the French and British inva-
    sions; she was sympathetic to the French,
    thereby a traitor to Queen Marie Caroline.

PINDARIC LADY: name for Elizabeth Rowe by Dunton.

PIOZZI: second married name of Hester Lynch
    Thrale.

PIPELET: first married name of Marie Theis de
    Constance, under T.

PISAN (PIZAN, PISA, PEZANO, PIZZANO): see Chris-
    tine de Pisan, under C.

PISCOPIA, CORNARO ELENE: 1646-1684; Venice, Ita-
    ly.
    Work: poems, Latin epistles, academic dis-
    courses, translations.
    She was a professor of philosophy, mathema-
    tics, theology, and astronomy. She was skil-

led in languages, music and poetry. She de-
cided, while still a child, against marriage,
as marriage was incompatible with her engros-
sing love of study. She was presented with a
wreath and laureate in the Duomo of Padua in
1678.

PIX, MARY (nee GRIFFITH): 1666-1720?; Oxford-
shire and London, England.
Work: *Ibrahim, the Thirteenth Emperor of the
Turks,* 1696, a blank verse tragedy; *Violenta,
or The Reward of Virtue, Turn'd from Bocacce
into Verse,* 1704; also novels and comedies.
She wrote poetry from childhood, but her re-
putation rests on plays; she married in 1684;
had one child, who died in 1690.

PLANEY, DE: see Agnes de Bragelongne de Planey,
under B.

POETESS, THE: popular name for Sappho. (Homer
was The Poet.) Also the nickname given Cath-
erine Gore by her childhood friends.

POLYHYMNIA: muse of sacred song.

PORDEN: maiden name of Eleanor Ann Franklin.

PORTER, ANNA MARIA: 1780-1832; Ireland, Scotland
and England. a.k.a. L'Alegro, by S.C. Hall.
Work: *Ballads and Romances and Other Poems,*
1811; *Artless Tales,* 1795, two volumes; also
plays, and fifty novels!
Educated at Edinburgh at thirteen she began
writing her tales which were published in
1795, 1797 and 1798 anonymously; her play
was acted in Covent Garden but was not suc-
cessful; most of her novels were translated
into French.

PORTER, SARAH: fl. 1791; United States.
Work: *The Royal Penitent, and David's La-
mentation over Saul and Jonathan,* 1791.

POST, ELIZABETH MARIA: 1755-1812; Netherlands.
Work: *Elegies,* 1794; *New Poems,* 1807; *Ge-
zangen der Liefde,* 1794.

POWER: maiden name of Sarah Helen Whitman.

PRAT, DU: married name of Anne de Seguier.

PRAXILLA: fl. 451, B.C.; Sicyon; Greece.
Work: dithyrambs, scolia (drinking songs) and

hymns.

PRECIEUSE: term applied to literary women of
France, especially during the 17th century;
began with Catherine de Vivonne, Marquise de
Rambouillet (1588-1665), who had a salon.

PREZ: see Sainte des Prez, under S.

PRIMROSE: middle name of Dorothea Campbell.

PRIMROSE, LADY DIANA: fl. 1630; England.
Work: *A Chain of Pearl*, 1630; by the "noble
Lady Diana Primrose."
Her identity is unknown; she might have been
Anne Clifford, the wife of Philip Herbert,
Earl of Pembroke and Montgomery.

PRINCE: maiden name of ELizabeth Oakes Smith.

PROBA, VALERIA FALCONIA: fl. 438; Rome, born in
Etruria.
Work: a Virgilian cento on books of the Old
and New Testaments, printed in Frankfort,
1541; also a history of Christ.
The wife of Adolphus, she is not to be con-
fused with Anicia Falconia Proba, or Valeria
Proba, the wife of Adelsius.

PROESSA, CONTESSE DE: pseudonym of Garsenda de
Forcalquier, under G.

PRUSSIAN SAPPHO: nickname for Anna Luise Karsch.

PUDENS, AULUS RUFUS: husband of Claudia Rufina.

PUYTENDRE: married name of Justin de Levi.

QUAKER DOLLEY, QUEEN DOLLEY, and QUEEN DOWAGER:
all nicknames for Dorothea Madison.

QUEEN OF POETRY: nickname for Clemence Isaure.

QUELLENCE: first married name of Catharine de
Parthenai, which was later changed to Soubise.

QUESTIERS, KATHARINA: 1637-1669; Netherlands.
a.k.a. Tesselschade Redivina.
Work: *Klioos Kraam*, 1656; *Lauwer-Strijt*,
1665, collaborated with Cornelia van der Veer.
Well versed in many arts, she also translat-
ed plays; her nickname is a reference to a
favorite Dutch poet, Maria Visscher.

RADCLIFFE, ANN (nee WARD): 1764-1823; London, England.
Work: *The Poems of Ann Radcliffe*, 1816, unauthorized; *Poems* 1834; and novels.
She had little formal education; she originated the Gothic novel, the most famous being *Mysteries of Udolpho*; she did all her writing in ten years, retired to a peaceful private life. Her first book of poems was taken by an editor from her novels; it was said her prose was poetry, and her poetry was prose.

RADZIWILLOWA, FRANCISZKA URSZULA, PRINCESS (nee WISNIOWIESKA): 1705-1753; Poland.
Work: *Listy do Meza*, 1728; *Przestragi Corce Majej*, 1738; also, sixteen plays.
She was the first to introduce Moliere into Polish Drama.

RAMIREZ DE SANTILLANA: see Juana Ines de la Cruz, under C.

RAMSEY: maiden name of Charlotte Lennox.

RATHBONE, HANNAH MARY (nee REYNOLDS): 1798-1879; Shropshire, Liverpool, England.
Work: *The Strawberry Girl, with Other Thoughts and Fancies in Verse*, 1852; also edited anthologies.
She was skilled in drawings which were published; initiated the autobiographical type of historical novel, published anonymously.

RAVIRA, FELETTO ELEONORA OF CASALE: fl. 1559; Italy.
Work: poems.
She was the wife of Feletto, Lord of Melazzo.

RAYMOND: maiden name of Sophia Burrell.

REEVE, CLARA: 1729-1807; Ipswich, England.
Work: *Poems*, 1769; novels, translation, critical essays.
Educated by her father, her first poetry appeared when she was fourty; her novels influenced Radcliffe and others.

RENATUS: second married name of Catharine de Parthenai.

REYNOLDS: maiden name of Hannah Mary Rathbone.

RHODES: maiden name of Katharine Augusta Ware.

RIGGS: maiden name of Anna Miller.

ROBERTS, EMMA: 1794?-1840; England and India.
Work: *Oriental Scenes, Dramatic Sketches & Tales with Other Poems,* 1830, Calcutta; second edition, 1832, London. She also edited periodicals, wrote history, biography, tales, local description, essays, and was a foreign correspondent.
She was a friend of L.E.L.: died at Poonah, India; was buried there near Maria Jane Jewsbury.

ROBINSON, MARY (nee DARBY): 1758-1800; England and France. a.k.a. Perdita, in letters to George IV; La Belle Anglaise, by Marie Antoinette; Laura Maria and Tabitha Bramble were her pseudonyms.
Work: *Sappho and Phaon,* series of sonnets, 1796; *The Mistletoe, A Christmas Tale,* verse, 1800; poems published 1775; two more volumes in 1791; more poems in 1803, 1806, 1826; also plays, tales and novels.
Educated by the sisters of Hannah More, she taught school, and married 1774; soon went to prison with her husband for debt, where she cared for their child and wrote poetry, published 1775; was an actress until 1780; had an affair with the Prince of Wales who soon dumped her; after a fight, she received £500 pension.

ROBINSON, MARY ELIZABETH: died 1818; England.
Work: *The Wild Wreath,* 1805; miscellaneous poetry; also a novel.
She was the daughter of Mary Robinson, above.

ROBINSON, THERESE ALBERTINE LOUISE (nee VON JACOB): 1797-1870; Germany, Russia, U.S.A. a.k.a. Talvi (Talvj) and Ernst Berthold, pseudonyms.
Work: *Life and Works of Mrs. Therese Robinson,* 1914; a prolific writer, she published poems, tales, translations, songs, and language studies.
She emigrated to the U.S. in 1828; published

in German and English.

ROCHES: see Desroches.

ROHAN, ANNE DE; 1580-1646; France.
Work: poetry.
The daughter of Catharine de Parthenai-Sou-
bise, it was said of her that she could have
been the greatest female poet of her age,
but her piety turned her talent into another
channel.

ROMAN SAPPHO: popular name for Sulpicia, 1st
century.

ROMANINA, LA: popular name for Marianna Benti-
Bulgarelli.

ROMANS: see Bieris de Romans, under B.

ROSE, SAINT: 1586-1617; Lima, Peru. a.k.a. The
Rose of Lima, and the Rose of Saint Mary.
Work: poetry.
She was the first canonized American saint;
lived her life in imitation of Saint Cather-
ine of Sienna; had mystical gifts, visions,
and revelations.

ROSERS, DE: see Guillelma de Rosers, under G.

ROSSEN HELENA VON: real name of Hrotsvitha.

ROSVITHA: modern spelling of Hrotsvitha.

ROWE, ELIZABETH (nee SINGER): 1674-1737; Somer-
setshire; England. a.k.a. Philomela, pseu-
donym; called Pindaric Lady by Dunton.
Work: *Poems on Several Occasions by Philo-
mela*, 1696; *The History of Joseph*, poem;
also meditation, moral pieces.
Began writing poetry at twelve; was skilled
in music and painting. She married in 1709,
was widowed six years later; spent the rest
of her life at Frome, where most of her writ-
ing was done.

ROWENA: pseudonym of Sophia Little.

ROWSON, SUSANNAH (nee HASWELL): 1762-1824; Lon-
don and U.S.A.
Work: *Poems on Various Subjects*, 1788; *A
Trip to Parnassus*, 1788, verse critique of
theater; *Miscellaneous Poems*, 1804, Boston;
also novels and comic operas.
She was an actress and educator as well as a

writer. Brought to the U.S. when she was
seven, she returned to England during the
Revolution; married, published novels, and
returned to the U.S. in 1793; worked as an
actress and opened a school for girls. Her
novel, *Charlotte, a Tale of Truth*, was Ameri-
ca's best seller before *Uncle Tom's Cabin*;
more than one hundred and sixty editions be-
fore 1905!

RUAIDH: see Mari Nighean Alisdair Ruaidh, under
M.

RUFINA, CLAUDIA: 100; Roman who lived in Bri-
tain.
Work: *An Elegy on her Husband's Death*; oth-
er poems, prose and epigrams.
Her husband was Aulus Rufus Pudens, a Bonon-
ian philosopher, a member of the Roman eques-
train order stationed in Britain.

RUSH: maiden name of Julia Ward.

RUSSELL: middle name of Mary Mitford.

RUSSELL, LADY: title of Lucy Harington, Count-
ess of Bedford.

RUTHERFORD: maiden name of Alicia (Alison)
Cockburn.

RUTLAND, COUNTESS: title of Elizabeth Manners.

SABLIERE, MARGUERITE (nee HEISEN): 1636-1693;
Paris, France.
Work: poems.
She was a friend of La Fontaine, who lived
in her house for twenty years. She later
retired to a convent.

SAINTE DES PREZ: 13th century, France.
Work: poems.
A pupil of Agnes de Bragelongne de Planey;
at the age of twelve, she met and fell in
love with an English gentleman aged thirty;
ten years later, they married but she died
soon after.

SAINTE-PHALIER, FRANCOISE THERESE AUMILE DE:
died 1757; Paris, France.
Work: *The Confident Rival*, comedy; poetry.

SAINT GEORGE: first married name of Melesina
    Trench.
SAKANOE, LADY: 700-750; Japan.
    Work: *A Maiden's Lament,* poem.
SALM-DYCK, PRINCESS: title of Constance de
    Theis during her second marriage.
SALUSBURY: maiden name of Hester Lynch Thrale.
SALUZZO, DIODATA: 1775-1840; Italy.
    Work: *Amazoni,* an epic, 1795; *Versi,* 1816-7;
    Poesie Postume, 1852; also tragedies and no-
    vels.
SANCHO PANZA IN PETTICOATS: name for Mary Mit-
    ford by Letitia Landon.
SAND, GOERGE: pseudonym and adopted name of Ma-
    rie Aurore Dudevant.
SAPPHIRA: nickname for Mary Barber, by Swift.
SAPPHO (SAPPHA, PSAPPHO): fl. 600 B.C.; Lesbos,
    Greece. a.k.a. The Tenth Muse, by Plato; The
    Poetess, and Pierian Bee, popular names.
    Work: eight books of poetry in fifty dif-
    ferent meters; only fragments survive; one
    complete poem, another nearly complete.
    She is the most quoted, copied, translated,
    and plagiarized female poet. Her work cir-
    culated for over one thousand years in the
    Greek and Roman worlds, until fanatic Chris-
    tians burned all her poetry along with other
    classical works. Modern editions of her
    poetry are too numerous to list here.
SAPPHO: many poets have been compared to Sappho;
    see: American Sappho, Arabian Sappho, Bra-
    bantine Sappho, Damse Sappho, De Furious Sap-
    pho, German Sappho, English Sappho, Negro
    Sappho, Roman Sappho, Second Sappho, Toulou-
    sian Sappho, and Madelein Scuderi.
SAUMAISE DE CHAZAN: maiden name of Charlotte
    Bregy.
SAVOI (SAVOY): see Margaret of Savoie, under M.
SCHACKLETON: maiden name of Mary Leadbeater.
SCHOLASTICA: nickname for Claude de Bector,
    under B.
SCHUBART: maiden name of Sophia Brentano.
SCHUYLER: maiden name of Ann Eliza Bleeker.

SCOTT, JULIA H. (nee KINNEY): died 1842; Penn-
sylvania.
Work: poems found in *The American Female
Poets*, edited by Caroline May.
SCOTTISH MINSTREL: pseudonym of Caroline Nairne.
SCUDERI (SCUDERY) MADELEIN: 1607-1701; Havre de
Grace, Paris, France. Called herself Sappho.
Work: *Carte de Tendre*, a famous romance;
also poems, and fables.
She had a salon at Paris; was chosen to suc-
ceed Helena Cornaro at the Academy of Ricov-
rati at Padua; received pensions from Chris-
tina of Sweden; Louis XIV and Cardinal Maza-
rin; she won the first prize for eloquence
bestowed by the Academy of Paris; her novels
were translated into all the Romance lang-
guages.
SECOND SAPPHO: popular name for Laura Ammanati.
SEGLA: maiden name of Jeanne de Montegut.
SEGUIER, ANNE DE: fl. 1573; France. a.k.a. Du
Prat, from her marriage to Baron de Thiers.
Work: poetry.
Her daughters, Anne and Philippine, were edu-
cated at the court of Henry III; were also
known for their literary abilities.
SEI SHONAGON: 966,7-1013; Japan. Pseudonym of
Nakika.
Work: *Makura No Soshi (The Pillow Book)*,
a diary of court life in poetical style.
She entered the service of Empress Sadako
in 1000.
SELENA: nickname for Lucy Harington by Drayton.
SELVOGGIA, RICCIARDA: 14th century; Pistoia,
Italy.
Work: madrigals.
She is called the Bel Numero Una (the Fair
Number One) of the four celebrated women of
the fourteenth century in Italy; from a a
noble family, her parents rejected Cino as
a suitor, but when the family was banished
for political reasons, Cino helped them, and
was thus accepted as her suitor. She died

soon after.

SEMPRONIA: pseudonym of Mary Lamb.

SERMENT, LOUISE ANASTASIE: 1642-1692; Grenoble, France.

Work: poems in French and Latin; operas in collaboration with Quinant.

She was a member of the Academy of Ricovrati at Padua; it is said the best parts of the operas of Quinant were her work.

SEWARD, ANN: 1742-1809; Derbyshire and Staffordshire, England. a.k.a. Swan of Lichfield, a popular name.

Work: *Louisa, a Poetical Novel,* 1782; *Sonnets,* 1789; *Poetical Works,* three volumes, edited by Sir Walter Scott, 1810.

At three, she was reading Milton and Shakespeare; at nine, she recited verbatim the first three books of *Paradise Lost.* She began writing verse at twelve. She was self-educated; her jealous father attempted to stop her writing poetry. She belonged to the literary circle at Anna Miller's home.

SEYMOUR SISTERS: ANNE, MARGARET AND JANE: mid-16th century; England.

Work: 104 Latin distichs on the death of Margaret of Navarre, Queen of France; translated into French, Greek, and Latin, and printed in Paris, 1551.

The three sisters were known for their poetry; Anne married the Earl of Warwick, later married Edward Hunter; Margaret and Jane stayed single; Jane was maid of honor to Queen Elizabeth; she died at twenty in 1560.

SHACKELFORD: maiden name of Anna Peyre Dinnies.

SHAO FEI-FEI: 17th century, Hsi Hu, China.

Work: found in *The Orchid Boat,* pp. 64, 132. Hsi Hu (West Lake) was noted for its beautiful scenery and people; an official paid a great sum of money to her mother to take her as a concubine; she later remarried, possibly because of the jealousy of the official's wife.

SHARPLESS: maiden name of Mira Townsend.

SHERIDAN, FRANCES (nee CHAMBERLAINE): 1724-1767;
    Ireland and London.
    Work: poetry, novels, comedies, a pamphlet
    defending theater.
    The youngest of five, her mother died soon
    after she was born; her older brothers taught
    her surreptitiously when her father refused
    to allow her to learn to read and write. At
    fifteen, she wrote a two volume romance, *Eu-
    genie and Adelaide;* attempted a sermon. When
    her father became insane, she began attend-
    ing the theater where she met and married
    Thomas Sheridan; her plays were successful.
SHIKIBU: see Izumi Shikibu, under I, or Mura-
    saki Shikibu, under M.
SHIKISHI, PRINCESS: died 1201; Japan.
    Work: tanka poetry.
    She was the daughter of ex-emperor Goshira-
    kawa.
SIBYL: female poet/prophets of the ancient world:
    Greece, Egypt, Persia, Babylon, Italy, and
    Israel.
SIBYL OF CUMAI: Ancient Italy, Camparia. a.k.a.
    Demo, Amalthea, Herophile, Demophile, Dei-
    phobe.
    Work: three Sibyline books, written on palm
    leaves in verse hieroglyphics, dating from
    the time of Tarquinius Priscus, or Tarquinius
    Superbus.
    These three books formed an important part
    in the history of Rome; they were consulted
    constantly and people abided by their ad-
    vice; they contained directions for the wor-
    ship of gods, and policies of Romans, writ-
    ten in Greek hexameters. The legend is that
    the Sibyl of Cumai brought nine books to the
    king, who refused to buy them; she destroyed
    three and offered the rest for the same
    price; when she had destroyed three more, the
    king finally bought the last three for the
    original price!
SIBYL OF THE RHINE: name for Hildegardis of
    Bingen, under H.

SIDNEY: maiden name of Mary Herbert, Elizabeth Manners, and Mary Wroth; all related, aunt and nieces.

SIGOURNEY, LYDIA (nee HUNTLEY): 1791-1865; Connecticut. a.k.a. Sweet Singer of Hartford, American Hemans, and Female Milton.
Work: *Moral Pieces in Prose and Verse*, 1815; *Poems, Religious and Elegiac*, 1841; sixty-seven volumes in all, mostly poetry; also, two thousand articles and verses contributed to three hundred periodicals.
Educated by her mother, she became a teacher at twenty; first published poetry at twenty-four. She wrote to supplement her husband's income, though all her poems published before 1830 were anonymous. She became the most widely read American poet before Longfellow; had a salon at Hartford; she was so popular, she was paid for the use of her name in *Godey's Ladies Book*.

SILLERY: maiden name of Marchioness De Tibergeau.

SILVANIA: pseudonym of Elisabeth Wolff-Bekker.

SILVEIRA BUENA, BARBARA DA: 18th century, Brazil.
Work: poems.
Caught in the conspiracy of 1789 to make Brazil independent, she died soon after her husband's deportation.

SINGER: maiden name of Elizabeth Rowe.

S.M.: another pseudonym of Caroline Nairne.

SMITH, ANN YOUNG: FL. 1786-1792; Philadelphia. a.k.a. Sylvia.
Work: poetry.

SMITH, CHARLOTTE (nee TURNER): 1749-1806; Surrey and London, England.
Work: *Sonnets and Other Essays*, 1784; *The Emigrants*, poem, 1793; *Elegiac Sonnets and Other Poems*, 1800, London; *Conversations, Introducing Poetry*, 1804.
Orphaned at three, erratically educated, she left school at twelve, married at fifteen, and had twelve children. She worked for her

father-in-law, who said she was better than all his male clerks. After separating from her husband, she wrote twenty books to support her children. Her novels attack slavery, defend oppressed women, plead for female education and autonomy. Her sister, Catherine Dorset, was also a poet.

SMITH, ELIZABETH: 1776-1806; Durham, England.
Work: *Fragments; Translation of Job*, and poetry.
She knew mathematics and drawing; Hebrew, Syriac, Arabic, Persian, Greek, Latin, Italian, Spanish, German, and French!

SMITH, ELIZABETH OAKES (nee PRINCE): 1806-1893; Maine. a.k.a. Ernest Helfenstein, Mrs. Seba Smith, and Oakes Smith, all pseudonyms.
Work: *The Sinless Child and Other Poems*, 1844; *Woman and Her Needs*, 1851, advocating suffrage; also novels, history, tragedy, essays, tales and criticism.
She kept a journal and an imaginary correspondence during childhood (begun at eight). Though she first published anonymously, she was the first woman in the U.S. to lecture publicly; she preached in churches, and had a pastorate in New York. She had five sons, was secretly glad not to have daughters because of the limitations imposed on women. She wrote to support her family.

SOLAR, MARIN DE: see Mercedes Marin de Solar, under M.

SOLZA: married name of Emilia Brambati.

SOMERSET, DUCHESS: title of Frances Thynne.

SOPHIA OF HISPALI: died 1039; Seville, Spain.
Work: poetry and oratory, none extant.
Sister of Maria of Hispali.

SOUBISE: first married name of Catharine de Parthenai.

SOUTHEY, CAROLINE ANNE (nee BOWLES): 1786-1854; Keswick and Hampshire, England. a.k.a. Cowper of our Modern Poetesses, by Henry Nelson Coleridge.
Work: *Ellen FitzArthur*, a metrical tale,

1820; *Poetical Works,* 1867.

She was educated by her father. Faced with poverty, she sent her first poem to Robert Southey; it was printed anonymously in 1820, thus beginning a twenty year correspondence with Southey. They married when she was fifty-three. Queen Victoria gave her a pension of two hundred pounds.

SPEGHT, RACHEL: fl. 1617-1621; England.

Work: *Mortalities Memorandum,* 1621; *a Mouzell for Melastomus,* 1617, a rebuttal to anti-feminism.

She may have been the daughter of Thomas Speght.

STAMPA, CASSANDRA: fl. 1525; Padua and Venice, Italy.

Work: poetry and songs.

Her sister Gaspara Stampa, and her brother Baldassare, also wrote songs and poetry; they all worked together.

STAMPA, GASPARA: 1523-1554; Padua and Venice.

Work: *Rime,* 1554; *Canzoniere.*

Called the greatest woman poet of the Renaissance, she spent most of her thirty-one years in Venice; fell in love with a count who tired of her, resulting in the most fervent, clear, and eloquent love poetry of Italy; her sister Cassandra and brother Baldassare were poets and singers with her.

STEELE, ANNE: 1717-1778; Hampshire, England. a. k.a. Theodosia, pseudonym.

Work: *Poems on Subjects Chiefly Devotional,* 1760; reprinted in 1780; *Hymns, Psalms and Poems by Anne Steele,* 1863; London.

Her fiance died by drowning a few hours before their wedding was to have taken place.

STELLA: name for Hannah More by Anne Yearsley.

STOCKTON, ANNE: fl. 1770's; Pennsylvania.

Work: a series of poems on liberty during the Revolutionary War.

STODDARD, LAVINIA (nee STONE): 1787-1820; Connecticut and Alabama.

Work: poems.

She had an academy at Troy, New York with her husband. Her most famous poem was *The Soul's Defiance.*

STONE: maiden name of Lavinia Stoddard.

STRICKLAND: family name of the four famous sisters, all writers, two of whom are poets: Susanna Moodie, and Catherine Parr Traill.

STROZZI (STROZZA): see Barbara Torelli-Strozzi, under T.

STUART: family name of Mary, Queen of Scots, under M.
Also the middle name of Louisa Costello.

SU HSAIO-HSAIO: late 5th century, Chekiang, China.
Work: found in *The Orchid Boat,* pp. 12, 132.
A legendary courtesan of Hang Chou, her tomb shrine still stands at West Lake; she is reputed to have been one of the two most beautiful women who ever lived.

SULEIKA: name for Marianne Von Willemer, by Goethe.

SULPICIA I: 64 B.C. to 8 A.D.; Rome, Italy.
Work: *No Harm to Lovers: the Love of Sulpicia and Cerinthus as Revealed in Six Poems by Sulpicia and Six Elegies by Albius Tibullus,* translated from Latin by Herbert Creekmore, 1950.
The niece and ward of Messala, she is not to be confused with her namesake, celebrated by Martian; her poetry is a unique reflection of the freedom enjoyed by young women of the upper classes at Rome in the Augustan Age.

SULPICIA II: first century, A.D.: Rome. a.k.a. Roman Sappho.
Work: an extant fragment, a satire against Domitian, usually found at the end of *Satires of Juvenal,* to whom it was falsely attributed.
The author of many poems, she was the first Roman woman who taught other women to vie with the Greeks in poetry; she wrote of honorable love.

SUN TAO-HSUAN: early 12th century, China.

Work: found in *The Orchid Boat*, pp. 51, 133. Widowed at thirty, she never remarried; when old, she burned all her poems, but her son collected some that had circulated in manuscript.

SUN YUN-FENG: 1764-1814; Chekiang, China.
Work: found in *The Orchid Boat*, pp. 68-71, and 133.
The daughter of an official, the wife of a scholar, she was one of the favorites among thirteen women students of the leading Ching Dynasty poet Yuan Mei.

SURVILLE, MARGUERITE ELEONORE CLOTILDE DE: 1405-1495; Lyon, France.
Work: *Poesies de Clotilde*.
Educated at court, at eleven she translated one of Petrarch's Canzoni. She married at sixteen; her husband was killed while fighting for Jeanne d'Arc at Orleans. She did not remarry; devoted herself to literature and the education of her son. She gained fame as a poet; Margaret of Scotland invited her to court but she refused.

SUZE, DE LA: second married name of Henrietta Coligny.

SWAN OF LICHFIELD: popular name for Anna Seward.

SWEDISH SEVIGNE: popular name for Baroness d' Albedyhl.

SWEET SINGER OF HARTFORD: popular name for Lydia Sigourney.

SYLVIA: penname of Ann Young Smith.

SYNBERRIE: name for Tullia D'Aragona, by Girolamo Muzio.

TABITHA BRAMBLE: pseudonym of Mary Robinson.

TAGGART, CYNTHIA: 1804-1849; Rhode Island.
Work: poems published in 1834, with an autobiography.
Her training was religious; after an illness at nineteen, she turned to writing, too weak to do anything else; was unable to sleep except with drugs, was ill all of her life.

TALVI (TALVJ): pseudonym of Therese Albertine
Louise von Jacob Robinson, using the first
letters of her given name.
TAMBRONI, CLOTILDE: 1758-1817; Bologna, Italy.
Work: poems in Greek; also translations
from Greek.
She was a professor of Greek at the University of Bologna; she delivered an oration in
Latin on the inauguration of Doctor Maria
Dalle-Donne into the college honors.
TANFIELD: maiden name of Elizabeth Carew
(Carey).
T'ANG WAN: 12th century, China.
Work: found in *The Orchid Boat,* pp. 50 and
133-4.
The first wife of Sung poet Lu Yu; her mother-in-law disliked her, and sent her away.
She then married a scholar, but she and her
first husband never stopped loving each
other; their love is the subject of their
poems.
TANSKA, CLEMENTINA: 1800 - ?; Warsaw, Poland.
Work: poetry and tales.
Her writings of Polish historical events
were popular.
TAOIST MASTER IN THE STRAW COAT: Wang Wei's
name for herself.
TASTU, SABINE CASIMIR AMABLE (nee VOIART [VOREST]): 1798-1885; Metz, France.
Work: *Poesies,* 1826; *Poesies Nouvelles,*
1834; also books for young children, stories,
educational books, and a translation into
French of *Robinson Crusoe* in 1835.
TAYLOR, ANN: 1782-1866; Suffolk and London, England. a.k.a. Gilbert, her married name.
Work: *Poetical Works by Ann and Jane Taylor,*
1877.
Ann was the first to write for publication;
at sixteen, won a prize for a verse solution
to a riddle; married in 1812, had many chilren; survived her sister by fourty-two
years; wrote hymns and autobiography.
TAYLOR, JANE: 1783-1824; Suffolk and London.

Work: *Original Poems for Infant Minds*,
1804-5, in collaboration with her sister,
Ann; this edition went through fifty Eng-
lish editions in their lifetime, was trans-
lated into European languages.
Jane and Ann were in the vanguard of the
movement for an appropriate literature for
the young; they were called inventors of the
"awful warning" school of poetry; Jane was
more humorous and jolly than Ann. She died
of tuberculosis at fourty; their work after
Ann's marriage and their separation was not
as good as in collaboration.

TAYLORS OF ONGAR: Ann and Jane Taylor with
their parents, all writers.

TELESILLA: fl. 510 B.C.: Argos, Greece.
Work: *De Telesillae Reliquiis*, the remain-
ing nine fragments of her poetry, edited by
Neue, 1843.
She inspired the Argive women to fight Cleo-
menes, the Spartan king, and later Demaratus
in the siege of Pamphiliacum; they were
victorious, and her statue was erected in
the temple of Aphrodite at Argos. Her hymns
to Apollo and Artemis used a meter since
then named for her: the telesilleion, or
acephalous glyconic. She wrote mainly for
women.

TENTH MUSE: a term of praise first applied to
Sappho, by Plato. Down through the years
since 300 B.C., many female poets have been
called the Tenth Muse in comparisons with
Sappho: Anne Bradstreet, Juana Ines de la
Cruz, Antoinette Desjoulieres, Catharine
Lescaile, Margaret of Navarre, and others.

TEODORO, DANTI: 1498-1573; Perugia, Italy.
Work: poems, a treatise on painting, a com-
mentary on Euclid.
She was a scholar of science, physics and
painting. She never married.

TERESA (THERESA) SAINT: 1515-1582; Avila and
Alba, Spain.
Work: *Obras Completas*, edited by Father

Odel Nino Jesus, and Father E. de la Madre de Dios, 1951, with a full bibliography; poetry, prose, autobiography.

At seven, she ran away from home, to be martyred by the Moors at Morocco; when her mother died, she was put in a nunnery at twelve; later, when her father refused to allow her to become a nun, she again left home secretly, and entered the Carmelite Convent at Avila. She took her vows in 1534; felt called to reform the Carmelite order; between 1562-1576, she established nine convents; at her death, there were thirty-two congregations of her order. Her prose visions, poetry and autobiography are an established part of Spanish literature.

TERRACINA, LAURA: 1519-1577; Naples, Italy.
Work: poetry published in Venice in 1548, four editions.
She was one of the most productive sixteenth century women poets.

TERRY, LUCY: 18th century, Massachusetts.
Work: a verse account of an Indian raid on Old Deerfield.
She was a slave who managed to learn to write; no other work of hers has been found.

TESSELSCHADE: nickname for Maria Visscher, by her father, which means Texel's Wreck, from one of his financial disasters.

TESSELSCHADE REDIVINA: name for Katharine Questiers, by those who compared her to Visscher.

THALIA: muse of pastoral poetry and comedy.

THALIA: nickname for Tullia D'Aragona, by Muzio.

THEANO OF CRETE: 6th century, B.C.; Greece.
Work: poetry.
Said by some to have been the wife of Pythagoras, she was a philosopher of the Pythagorean school.

THEANO LOCRENCIS: no date, Ancient Greece. a.k.a. Melica.
Work: songs, lyric poems.
She was surnamed Melica from the melody of her songs and poems.

THEIS DE CONSTANCE, MARIE (PRINCESS OF SALM-
    DYCK): 1767 - ?; Nantes, Paris, France and
    Germany. a.k.a. Pipelet, her first married
    name.
    Work: ballads with melodies, piano accom-
    paniments, poetical epistles, dramas and
    verse; and a four-act opera in verse, *Sappho*.
    She married Pipelet 1789; they lived in Pa-
    ris. She married Count de Salm-Dyck in
    1803; after 1816, they lived in Germany as
    well as Paris.
THEODOSIA: pseudonym of Anne Steele.
THERESA, SAINT: see Teresa.
THIERS, BARONESS: title of Anne de Seguier.
THOMAS, ELIZABETH: 1677-1731; England. a.k.a.
    Corinna, a pseudonym.
    Work: *Poems on Several Occasions, by a
    Lady,* 1722; also letters.
    She sold twenty-five letters of Pope to
    Curll, who printed them in 1726; she may
    have blackmailed Pope; was sent to prison
    for debt; while there, she wrote a ficti-
    tious description of the death of Dryden to
    make money.
THOMSON: maiden name of Janet Hamilton.
THRALE, HESTER LYNCH (nee SALUSBURY): 1741-1821;
    Carnarvonshire, London, England. a.k.a. her
    second married name, Piozzi.
    Work: *Autobiography, Letters and Literary
    Remains,* 1861, two volumes; *Thraliana,* 1951,
    edited by K. Balderston.
    The only child of an unhappy marriage, she
    was married against her will to Thrale; they
    had twelve children. In 1764, she met Dr.
    Johnson, became his closest friend; he prac-
    tically lived in their house until Thrale
    died in 1781. Instead of marrying Johnson,
    she then married Piozzi, which caused a
    stormy controversy; nevertheless, she was
    happily married for the next twenty-five
    years. *Thraliana* has been called "an un-
    conscious piece of realistic self-portrait-
    ure of high value."

THYMELE: reign of Domitian, Greece.
 Work: poetry and music.
 She was also an actress (mima). She is re-
 ported to have been the first to introduce
 into Greek theater a kind of dance called a
 Themelinos; also named for her was an altar
 used in theaters.
THYNNE, FRANCES (DUCHESS OF SOMERSET): died
 1754; England. a.k.a. Cleora and Eusebia,
 pseudonyms.
 Work: poetry.
 Tending her sick husband took up most of
 her life; she was fond of literary society,
 a friend of Elizabeth Rowe.
TIAN: pseudonym of Karoline Gunderode.
TIBBY: nickname for Isobel Pagan.
TIBERGEAU, MARCHIONESS DE (nee SILLERY): 17th
 century, France.
 Work: poetry.
 She was a patron of literature; died at the
 age of eighty.
TIBORS: c. 1130; Provence, France.
 Work; found in *The Women Troubadours*, pp.
 80-81, and 162.
 She was probably the earliest of the women
 troubadours; wife of Bertand de Baux, she was
 twice married by twenty; had three sons, died
 at fifty-two; was guardian of the leading
 troubadour, her younger brother, Raimbaut
 d'Orange.
TIGHE, MARY (nee BLACKFORD): 1772-1810; Wick-
 low, Ireland.
 Work: *Psyche, or the Legend of Love*, 1795-
 1805; *Psyche and Other Poems*, 1811, reprint.
 Her poem *Psyche* was so successful, even
 though printed by friends, that she was able
 to build an addition to an orphan asylum in
 Wicklow, thereafter called the Psyche Ward.
 She was not happily married, had no children,
 died of consumption at thirty-eight.
TODD: first married name of Dorothea Madison.
TOLLET, ELIZABETH: 1694-1754; London, England.
 Work: *Poems on Several Occasions, with Anne*

Boleyn to King Henry VIII, an Epistle, 1755; poems in Latin and English.
Raised in the Tower of London, where her father was commissioner of the Navy, she was well-educated by her father. She never married.

TOMLINS, ELIZABETH: 1768-1826; London, England.
Work: poetry, tales, novels, translations.
Wrote poetry while young; as an adult, she mostly wrote prose.

TOMPSON: maiden or middle name of Anna Tompson Hayden.

TONNA, CHARLOTTE ELIZABETH (nee BROWNE): 1790-1846; Norwich, England. a.k.a. Phelan, her first married name, and Charlotte Elizabeth, pseudonym.
Work: *The Wrongs of Women in Four Parts,* 1833-4, London; *Works of Charlotte Elizabeth,* three volumes, second edition 1845; seventh edition, 1849, both in New York.
She lived at Nova Scotia for a time with Phelan; they separated in 1824; she married Tonna in 1841. Her tracts against the Roman Catholic Church were listed on the R.C.C. Index Expurgatorius.

TORELLI-BENEDETTI, BARBARA: 1546-1598; Italy.
Work: *Partenia,* pastoral drama in blank verse; sonnets.

TORELLI-STROZZI, BARBARA: 1475-1533, Quastalla and Bologna, Italy. a.k.a. Benti-Voglio, her first married name.
Work: poetry.
She was married in 1491, but fell in love with Strozza, which caused a scandal; legally separated from her husband, she married her lover in 1507; he was murdered a year later by the Benti-Voglios; her poem on the death of Strozza is one of the best ever written from that culture.

TORNABUONI, LUCREZIA: 1425-1482; Florence, Italy.
Work: *Laude,* hymns in Italian.

The gifted, spiritual center of the Medici family, she was also a patron of arts and letters. She was adviser to her husband, Piero, and son, Lorenzo the Magnificent; she had three daughters and two sons, whom she brought up in strict accordance with the church (which they never abandoned).

TORRELLA, IPPOLITA: fl. 1500's; Reggio, Italy.
a.k.a. Castigliona, her married name.
Work: poems in Latin.
She was a friend of Olimpia Morati.

TOSINI, EUTROPIA: no date; Ferrara, Italy.
Work: poems in the collection by Bergalli.
A nun of the Augustine Order, her work was suppressed by the censors as being detrimental to the Church.

TOULOUSIAN SAPPHO: popular name for Clemence Isaure.

TOWNSEND, ELIZA PARKER: 1789-1854; Boston, Massachusetts.
Work: religious poems published anonymously in periodicals.
The authorship of her poems was kept a secret for many years; she lived to sixty-five; made her home in Boston, and never married.

TOWNSEND, MIRA (nee SHARPLESS): 1798-1859; Philadelphia, Pennsylvania.
Work: *Reports and Realities from the Sketch Book of a Manager*, 1855, privately printed; also poetry printed in periodicals.
She married in 1828 and had six children. She was a philanthropist; promoted a public meeting of women to consider the abolition of capital punishment in 1847; she worked extensively for down-and-out women, anti-slavery, and prohibition.

TRAILL, CATHERINE PARR (nee STRICKLAND): 1802-1899; England and Canada.
Work: *Pearls and Pebbles*, 1894, biographical notes; *Studies of Plant Life in Canada*, 1885, also novels.
She was privately educated at home. She married in 1832, emigrated to Ontario, had nine

children; she was the first of the four fa-
mous Strickland sisters to appear in print.
TRENCH MELESINA (nee CHENEVIX): 1768-1827;
Ireland. a.k.a. St. George, her first mar-
ried name.
Work: *Mary Queen of Scots, an Historical
Ballad and Other Poems*, privately printed;
Campaspe, an Historical Tale and Other Poems,
1815.
She spent nearly twenty years traveling in
Germany, France and Italy; her husband
Trench was imprisoned in France by Napoleon;
they escaped in 1807 and lived the rest of
their lives in Dublin.
TROTTER: maiden name of Catharine Cockburn.
TROUBADOURESSE, LA: nickname for Barbe de Ver-
rue.
TROYES, DE: see Doete de Troyes, under D.
TS'AI YEN: 162?-239?; China.
Work: found in *The Orchid Boat*, pp. 4-7,
and 134.
She is considered the first great woman poet
in Chinese history; about 195 A.D., a widow,
she was captured by Huns and taken north to
become a concubine of a chieftain, had two
sons; she was later ransomed by Ts'ao, but
she had to leave her sons with the Huns.
TUDOR: family name of Queen Elizabeth I of Eng-
land.
TURRELL, JANE (nee COLMAN): 1708-1738; Massachu-
setts.
Work: *Reliquiae Turellae*, 1735; *Memoirs of
the Life and Death of the Pious and Ingenius
Mrs. Jane Turell*, 1735.
Began writing poetry at eleven, later kept a
religious diary; married in 1726, had four
children, three of whom died in infancy. The
fourth lived only eighteen months after her.
She died before she was thirty. Her husband
suppressed her poems of wit and humor out of
religious conviction.
TURENNE, DE: maiden name of Maria de Ventadorn.
TURNER: maiden name of the sisters Catherine

Dorset and Charlotte Smith.

TURNER, ELIZABETH: 1774-1846; Whitechurch, Eng-
    land.
    Work: poetry and children's books.
    She wrote moral tales in verse for children
    which she called cautionary stories; the
    heroes and heroines were all flowers; her
    books were popular in the 19th century.

TUTHILL, LOUISA CAROLINE (nee HUGGINS): 1798,9-
    1879; Connecticut, New York and New Jersey.
    Work: poems published anonymously in per-
    iodicals; wrote or edited thirty volumes,
    some specifically for women, some for child-
    ren; tales, stories; guides to manners,
    housekeeping, and child care; aesthetics,
    spiritual, and the first history of archi-
    tecture in the United States.
    She married young; her husband submitted her
    first poem for publication without her know-
    ledge. Widowed in 1825, with four children,
    she turned to writing to support herself.

TZU YEH: 3rd-4th centuries, China.
    Work: found in *The Orchid Boat*, pp. 9-10,
    and 133.
    There may have been an original Tzu Yeh, but
    most of the fourty-two poems attributed to
    her are popular folk songs of the Wu pro-
    vince.

URANIA: Spencer's name for Mary Herbert.

V: pseudonym of Caroline Clive.

VALERIA FALCONIA PROBA: listed under P.

VALMORE: married name of Marceline Desbordes-
    Valmore, under D.

VALOIS, MARGARET OF: see Margaret of France,
    1552-1615; or Margaret of Navarre, 1492-1549.

VEER, CORNELIA VAN DER: 17th century, Nether-
    lands.
    Work: *Lauwer-Struijt*, 1665, in collabora-
    tion with Katharina Questiers.

VENTADORN: see Maria de Ventadorn, under M.

VERDIER, MADAME DE: fl. 1769; Uzes, France.
Work: *The Bondage of Love*, an epistle in verse; other poems.
Her work was recognized by the Academy of Toulouse, 1769.

VERRUE: see Barbe de Verrue, under B.

VICHY, DE: maiden name of Marie de Vichy-Chamrond, Marquise du Deffand, under D.

VICOMTE DE LAUNAY, LE: pen name of Delphine Girardin and her husband.

VIGNE, ANNE DE LA: 1634-1684; Normandy, France.
Work: poetry.
She was a scientist as well as a poet; was a member of the Rocovrati Academy at Padua; She was a friend of Madelein de Scuderi and Mary Dupre. It is said she died of a disease brought on by an extreme devotion to study.

VILLANDON: see Marie Jeanne L'Heritier, under H.

VILLEDIEU, MARIE CATHARINE HORTENSE DE: 1632-1683; Alencon, France. a.k.a. De Chatte, her second married name; Des Jardins, her third married name.
Work: ten duodecimo volumes published in 1702; poetry, dramas, fables, romances, and short stories.
Her maiden name was des Jardins; she married Villedieu, then de Chatte, then a cousin, des Jardins.

VIOLANTE: see Violante do Ceo, under C.

VIOT, MARIE ANNE HENRIETTE (nee L'ESTANG): 1746-1802; Prussia and France. a.k.a. her first married name d'Autremont, second married name de Bourdic; her third husband's name was Viot.
Work: poetry, romances, opera.
She moved to France as a child; was married first at twelve. She had a seat in the Academy of Nismes.

VIRGIN MARY: popular name for Mary, the mother of Jesus.

VISSCHER, ANNA ROEMER: 1583-1649; Amsterdam,

Netherlands.

Work: *Poetical Works*, 1881; editor, N. Beets.
Married von Wesel, sister of Maria Visscher.

VISSCHER, MARIA: 1594-1649, Amsterdam,
Netherlands. a.k.a. Tesselschade by her
father; Eusebia, by Vondel. (She married
Krombalgh of Alkmaar.)

Work: *Tesselschade Jaarboekje*, 1838-1840;
three volumes.

Named for a financial disaster of her fath-
er's (Texel's Wreck), the name Tesselschade
nevertheless became associated with four of
the greatest writers in Dutch literature.
She wrote poetry all her life; in 1630 was
awarded a prize for her poetry; was consi-
dered one of the finest women poets of Hol-
land. She was called by the Dutch, Our Fair
Morality, Mirror of All Intelligent Minds,
and the Glory of our Country.

VOIART (VOREST): maiden name of Sabine Casimir
Amable Tastu, under T.

WALES, MARIA JAMES: fl. 1795; New York.

Work: found in *The Female Poets of America*,
edited by Caroline May.

She came to the U.S. at the age of seven.

WALLADA: early 5th century, Spain.

Work: poetry.

She was the daughter of Caliph al-Mustakfi,
was loved by the poet Ibn-Zaydun.

WANG CH'ING-HUI: end 13th century, Hang Chou,
China.

Work: found in *The Orchid Boat*, pp. 52, 134.

She was possibly a superintendant of cere-
monies of the Women's Quarters during the
last emperors of the Sung Dynasty; in 1276,
when Kublai Khan took Hang Chou, she was
carried away to the north with other palace
women.

WANG WEI: 17th century, Yang Chou, China.

Work: found in *The Orchid Boat*, pp. 65 and
134-5.

Orphaned at seven, she grew up to be a cour-
tesan and poet; she married twice; after her
husbands died, she became a priestess, cal-
ling herself the Taoist Master in the Straw
Coat. She traveled with her library on a
boat through the waterways of central China;
was considered one of the great nature poets.

WARD: maiden name of Ann Radcliffe.

WARD, JULIA (nee RUSH): fl. 1812; United States.
Work: found in *Female Poets of America*, edi-
ted by Rufus Griswold.
She was married in 1812.

WARDLAW, ELIZABETH (LADY) (nee HALKET): 1677-
1727; Scotland.
Work: *Hardyknute*, poem, 1719.
She first circulated *Hardyknute* as a frag-
ment of an ancient ballad she claimed to
have discovered, but friends maintained that
she was the author; she may also have writ-
ten or amended *Sir Patrick Spens*.

WARE, KATHARINE AUGUSTA (nee RHODES): 1797-1843;
Massachusetts.
Work: *Bower of Taste*, which she edited,
1828-30; *The Power of the Passions, and Oth-
er Poems*, 1842; also, poems in periodicals.
She married in 1819, went to Europe in 1831;
lived in Paris.

WARREN, MERCY (nee OTIS): 1728-1814; Massachu-
setts. a.k.a. Philomela.
Work: *Poems, Dramatic Miscellaneous*, 1790;
*The History of the Rise, Progress and Termi-
nation of the American Revolution with Bio-
graphical, Political and Moral Observations*,
1805, three volumes; other poetry and plays.
She was educated by local clergymen, mar-
ried in 1754; her husband encouraged her ta-
lents; she had five children; wrote satires
against the Tories, and helped crystallize
liberal opinion for the Revolution; she
wrote the first history of the American Revo-
lution; insisted in the rights of women to
have other than domestic concerns, and that
the problems of women were not inherited,

but educational.

WARWICK, LADY: title of Anne Seymour.

WATHEN: maiden name of Marianne Baillie.

WEBER: maiden name of Sofia Elisabeth Brenner.

WEI, LADY: late 11th, early 12th centuries, China.
> Work: found in *The Orchid Boat*, pp. 35, 135. She was considered one of the two best Sung women poets, along with Li Ch'ing-Chao.

WELLS, ANNA MARIA (nee FOSTER): 1794 - ?; Massachusetts.
> Work: found in *The American Female Poets*, edited by Caroline May.
> She was a sister of Frances S. Osgood, a later poet.

WELSH: middle name of Jane Carlyle.

WENTWORTH: middle name of Sarah Morton.

WESEL, VON: married name of Anna Roemer Visscher.

WEST, JANE: 1758-1852; London, England.
> Work: before 1800, she published six volumes of poetry, two tragedies, a comedy and two novels; also wrote plays.
> Self-educated, she began writing verse at thirteen. When she married West, she attended to household and dairy duties but did not assume the role of a servant. Her prose indicates a dislike of Wollstonecraft's ideas.

WESTON, ELIZABETH JANE: 1582-1612; England and Bohemia. a.k.a. Leon, her married name.
> Work: *Poemata*, 1602; *Parthenicon*, 1606; *Opuscula*, 1723.
> Skilled in languages, she wrote prose and verse in Latin; was considered one of the best Latin poets of the 16th century; wrote to support her family of seven children.

WHARTON, ANNE (COUNTESS) (nee LEE): 1632?-1685; Oxfordshire, England. a.k.a. Chloris, by Waller.
> Work: *Whartoniana*, 1727; poetry and plays.
> Married in 1673, she brought a dowry of ten thousand pounds and an annual pension of

two thousand five hundred; they were child-
less; she was unhappy, and tried to leave her
unfaithful husband.

WHEATLEY, PHILLIS: 1753-1784; Africa and Massa-
chusetts. a.k.a. Peters, her married name,
and The Negro Sappho.

Work: *Poems on Various Subjects, Religious
and Moral*, 1773, London; and *The Poems of
Phillis Wheatley*, 1966.

Purchased off the Boston slave market when
she was about six, the Wheatley family recog-
nized her ability and educated her; within
sixteen months, she could read the Bible in
English; she was a pet of the upper classes
of Boston. She was invited to England by
the Countess of Huntingdon, where her poems
were published; the book went through seven
editions in thirty years. She married a
free Negro and had three children; they were
poor, and she and all her children died by
the time she was thirty-one. Her poem to
George Washington contains the first refer-
ence to America as the land of Columbia.

WHITE: maiden or middle name of Sarah Livermore.

WHITMAN, SARAH HELEN (nee POWER): 1803-1878;
Rhode Island. a.k.a. Helen, and Egeria,
pseudonyms.

Work: *Poems*, 1878, Boston; *Hours of Life &
Other Poems*, 1853.

She was educated by her mother; married in
1828; lived in Boston; after her husband's
death, she returned to Providence. She was
engaged to Poe for awhile; after his death,
she was his apologist, using the pseudonym
of Egeria for critical essays.

WHITNEY, ISABELLA: fl. 1567-1573; England.

Work: *A Sweet Nosegay or Pleasant Posye Con-
taining a Hundred and Ten Phylosophicall
Flowers*, 1573; *The Copie of a Letter, Lately
Written in Meeter by a Yonge Gentlewoman; to
her Unconstant Lover. With an Admonition to
All Yong Gentilwomen, and to All Other Mayds
in General to Beware of Mennes Flattery*, 1567.

WIDOW KNIGHT: popular name for Sarah Kemble Knight.

WILLARD, EMMA (nee HART): 1787-1870; Connecticut and Vermont. a.k.a. Yates, her second married name.
Work: *Motive Powers which Produce the Circulation of the Blood,* a treatise; also, poems, and textbooks on history, geography, and education.
Self-educated, she spent her entire life promoting education for women; she founded Troy Female Seminary, and introduced modern teaching methods and trained teachers. Her work undoubtedly altered the course of American life; she threw away the rod, determined to interest pupils. In 1814, no college in the world admitted women! Hundreds of teachers were trained by her and sent south and west carrying the message of education for women. She was ridiculed for proposing the education of women; Troy Female Seminary is now named for her: Emma Willard School.

WILLEMER, MARIANNE VON (nee JUNG): 1798 - ?; Frankfurt-am-Main, Germany. a.k.a. Suleika, by Goethe.
Work: *West-Eastern Divan,* by Goethe, contains two of her poems.
Orphaned, she met von Willemer while traveling with a ballet group; she married him after his first wife died. Her relationship with Goethe was a distant but deep friendship: she admitted collaborating on the *West-Eastern Divan.*

WILLIAMS, ANNA: 1706-1783; South Wales and London, England.
Work: published poetry and prose; also translations.
She moved to London in 1730; became blind; lived with the Johnsons until her death.

WILLIAMS, CATHARINE READ (nee ARNOLD): 1790-1872; Rhode Island.
Work: *Original Poems on Various Subjects,* 1828, by subscription; *Tales, National &*

Revolutionary, 1830-35, two volumes.
Married in 1824, she bore one daughter and adopted a son; began teaching in 1826; divorced after two years, she turned to writing to support herself and was successful.

WILLIAMS, HELEN MARIA: 1762-1827; England and France.
Work: *An Ode to Peace, and Other Poems*, 1782-1788; also novels, and letters from France, eight volumes.
Settled in France 1790; sympathetic to the Girondists, she was imprisoned in 1794; she escaped to Switzerland and returned to Paris in 1796. She was the chief English witness to the French Revolution, although her information was not always reliable; later she was a part of Dr. Johnson's circle.

WILMOT: first married name of Barbarina Brand.

WINCHILSEA, COUNTESS: title of Anne Finch.

WINTER, LUCRETIA WILHELMINA (nee VAN MERKEN): 1721-1789; Leyden, Netherlands.
Work: *Het Nut der Tegenspoeden*, 1762; *David*, an epic, 1767; *Germanicus*, an epic, 1779; also plays.
She wrote nature poetry.

WISNIOWIESKA: maiden name of Franciszka Urszula Radziwillowa.

WOLF, ARNOLDINA: 1769-1820; Germany.
Work: poetry published in 1788.
At eighteen, she was attacked by a disease, and could not sleep for twenty-six weeks; she repeated and composed poetry to relieve her suffering; later she fell into insensibility but could hear; she was in constant dread of being buried alive, began to recover after four weeks. She married in 1791 and had nine children. Her poems and an account of her illness were published by Dr. Wiss.

WOLFE, BETJE: see Wolff-Bekker.

WOLFF-BEKKER, ELISABETH (nee WOLFE): 1738-1804; The Hague, Netherlands. a.k.a. Betje and Silvania, pseudonyms.
Work: fifteen volumes of poetry; novels,

essays and translations (ten alone and five with Agathe Dekken).

She eloped at seventeen but soon thought better of it; five years later, she married a clergyman thirty years older than she; with Dekken, she wrote the first Dutch domestic novels; they were refugees in France between 1788-1798 and lost their fortunes; they had to write to support themselves.

WOOD, JEAN (nee MONCURE):   fl. 1811; Scotland and Virginia.

Work: poetry.

She wrote enough poetry for a small volume; taught herself to play guitar and piano and to repair the spinet. Her only daughter became mentally ill at four and died at eighteen. Jean was a social reformer and founded the Female Humane Association of the City Richmond.

WOODBRIDGE, MERCY (nee DUDLEY): 1621-1661; Massachusetts and England.

Work: poems.

She was a sister of Anne Bradstreet; married in 1639 and had twelve children; lived in England between 1647-1663; her husband had Bradstreet's first book published while in England.

WORDSWORTH, DOROTHY: 1771-1855; England.

Work: *The Poetry of Dorothy Wordsworth Edited from Her Journals,* 1940, edited by J. Eigerman; *Journals,* published in 1896.

Overshadowed by her brother William and her own journals, her poetry is only now being recognized for its quality. She was orphaned at six; raised with other orphaned cousins; had very little formal education; her life was spent in companionship with William and their friends, traveling and writing.

She was insane her last twenty years.

WORTLEY: middle name of Mary Montague.

WREAKS: maiden name of Barbara Hofland.

WRENCH: maiden name of Margaret Holford.

WRIGHT, SUSANNA: 1697-1784; England and Wright's

Ferry, Pennsylvania. Called Philomel, by
James Logan.
Work: poetry.
She was also a legal counselor, an innkeep-
er and amateur physician. She came to Amer-
ica in 1714; when her mother died in 1722,
she became head of the household. She never
married; her house was a lodging place at
Wright's Ferry which her family controlled.
She made silk from her own cocoons on her
own mulberry trees; at one time, had one
thousand five hundred silkworms. She was a
scribe, and wrote deeds and wills, and acted
as counselor for her neighbors, judging dis-
putes. She understood apothecary; wrote pam-
phlets in defense of Indians, and had a large
library. She knew French, Italian, Latin and
natural philosophy.
WROTH, MARY (nee SIDNEY) (COUNTESS OF MONTGOMERY)
1586? - 1640?; England.
Work: *The Countess of Montgomeries Urania*,
1621.
She was a niece of Mary Herbert and a cousin
of Elizabeth Manners. She married at eigh-
teen, was often at court, a patron of poets.
The death of her husband left her with a
large debt; she wrote *Urania* as a financial
venture; it is a prose romance interspersed
with verse.
WU TSAO: 1800 - ?; China.
Work: found in *The Orchid Boat*, pp. 72-78,
135.
The daughter of one merchant, wife of anoth-
er, ill-treated by both, she soon lost int-
erest in males, had many female friends and
lovers; wrote erotic poems to courtesans.
She was very popular in her lifetime; in
1837, she became a Taoist priestess; she is
regarded as the third great woman poet of
China, after Li Ch'ing-Chao and Chu Shu-Chen.
WU TSE-T'IEN, EMPRESS: 624-705, China.
Work: found in *The Orchid Boat*, pp. 14 and
136-7.

She was the only Empress to rule alone in
Chinese history. She became a servant of the
Emperor T'ai, and worked her way up to the
throne through concubinage and murder. She
ruled alone from 689-705 after years of rul-
ing through her husband and son; after her
husband's death she openly kept a male har-
em. China thrived under her rule.
WYCKE, VAN: middle name of Margaretta Faugeres.

YALE: maiden name of Anne Hopkins.
YATES: second married name of Emma Willard.
YEARSLEY, ANNE: 1756-1806; Bristol and London,
England. a.k.a. Lactilla, and Bristol Milk-
woman.
Work: *Poems on Several Occasions,* fourth
edition, 1786; *Poems on Various Subjects and
Other Pieces,* 1787; *Poem on the Inhumanity
of the Slave Trade,* 1788; also an historical
tragedy and a novel.
The daughter of a milkwoman, and a milkwoman
herself, she was nicknamed Lactilla. She
married young to an illiterate man and had
six children. Hannah More helped publish
her poetry by subscription.
YORK: see Elizabeth of York, under E.
YTHA, SAINT: another spelling for Saint Ita.
YU HSUAN-CHI: died 870; Ch'ang An, China.
Work: found in *The Orchid Boat,* pp. 17-20;
137.
The concubine of an official, she was first
tortured by his wife and then driven from the
house. She became a Taoist priestess, trav-
eled widely, and had many lovers, including
poets. She was accused of murdering her
maid; in spite of the efforts of her friends
who tried to save her, she was executed.

ZAPPI, FAUSTINA (nee MARATTI): died 1740; Rome,
Italy.
Work: sonnets.

She was married to a poet; her poetry was
thought to have been better than his.
ZUZORIC, CRIJETA: c. 1555 - c. 1600; Italy.
Work: sonnets, epigrams.
She was believed to have written sonnets and
epigrams but none survive. She was also a
patron of literature.

ANTHOLOGIES OF WOMEN'S POETRY

20th Century:

From Deborah and Sappho to the Present: An Anthology of Women Poets, compiled by Anca Vrbovska and Alfred Dorn; edited by Mildred Wiackley; New York, New Orlando Publications, 1976.

The Women Troubadours, edited by Meg Bogan; New York, Paddington Press Ltd./Two Continents Publishing Group, 1976.

Salt and Bitter and Good: Three Centuries of English and American Women Poets, edited by Cora Kaplan, New York; Paddington Press Ltd,/ Two Continents Publishing Group, 1975.

The World Split Open, Four Centuries of Women Poets in England and America, 1552-1950; edited by Louise Bernikow, New York; Vintage Books Edition, 1974.

The Orchid Boat, Women Poets of China, translated and edited by Kenneth Rexroth and Ling Chung, New York; McGraw-Hill Book Company, 1972.

The Women Poets in English: An Anthology, edited by Ann Stanford, New York; McGraw-Hill Book Company, 1972.

The Distaff Muse: An Anthology of Poetry Written by Women, compiled by Clifford Bax and Meum Stewart, London; Hollis and Carter, 1949.

The Answering Voice: One Hundred Love Lyrics by Women, compiled by Sara Teasdale, New York; The MacMillan Company, 1926.

20th Century reprints of 19th Century Books:

Woman's Record, by Sarah Josepha Hale, New York; Source Book Press, 1970 (Reprint of 1855 Harper and Brothers edition); although this book is not an anthology, it contains more poetry

than any of the 20th century collections.
The American Female Poets, edited by Caroline
May, New York; Garrett Press, Inc. 1969.
(Reprint of the 1854 Lindsay and Blakiston
edition.)

19th Century:

The Female Poets of America, edited by Rufus
Griswold, Philadelphia; Carey and Hart, 1849.
The Female Poets of America, edited by Thomas
Buchanan Read, Philadelphia; E.H. Butler and
Company, 1849.
The British Female Poets, edited by George Wash-
ington Bethune, Philadelphia; Lindsay and
Blakiston, 1848.

BIOGRAPHICAL REFERENCES ON WOMEN

The Book of Women's Achievements, compiled by Joan Macksey and Kenneth Macksey, New York; Stein and Day, 1976.

Woman and her Master, by Lady Sydney Owenson Morgan, Connecticut; Hyperion Press, Inc. 1976 (reprint of 1840 edition).

Herstory: A Woman's View of American History, by June Sochen, New York; Alfred Publishing Company, Inc. 1974.

Notable American Women: 1607-1950, A Biographical Dictionary by Edward James, Janet Wilson James and Paul Boyer, Cambridge, Massachusetts; Belknap Press, of Harvard University Press, 1971; second edition 1973, three volumes.

Index to Women, by Norma Olin Ireland, Massachusetts; F.W. Faxon Company, Inc., 1970.

Women's Record, by Sarah Josepha Hale, New York; Source Book Press, 1970 (reprint of 1855 edition, Harper and Brothers).

A Woman of the Century: 1400 Biographies of Leading American Women, edited by Frances E. Willard and Mary A. Livermore, Detroit; Gale Research Company, 1967 (reprint of Charles Wells Moulton Publisher edition, 1893).

Remember the Ladies: The Story of Great Women Who Helped Shape America, by Emily Taft Douglas, New York; G.P. Putnam's Sons, 1966.

These Were the Women: U.S.A. 1776-1806, by Mary Ormsbee Whitton, New York; Hastings House, 1954.

Ladies of Literature, by Laura L. Hinkley, New York; Hastings House, 1946.

Daughters of America or Women of the Century, by Phebe A. Hanaford, Maine; True and Company, circa 1883.